MW01035053

FAIR WINDS, FOLLOWING SEAS,
and a Few Bolters

"The inspiring story of a US Navy carrier pilot's life, truly lived as a 'daring adventure.' I have yet to read a more honest portrait of an American patriot."

—**Bob Dorgan**, USN Veteran, author of *Sea Pay: An Enlisted Man's Naval Adventure*

"Honest and compelling—a MUST read!
"Steve McKenna's autobiography is an in-depth look at what hard work and determination can get you. He takes you on a journey that is both relatable and informative. His time as a naval aviator is uniquely crafted with true insight into the operations and mindset of Navy life. The fearless writing will draw you in and give you a glimpse at Steve's passions, dreams, successes, and failures. If you are looking for a well-told story with an honest backbone look no further."

—**Brent Ladd Loefke**, author of the *Codi Sanders* series

"Stephen McKenna gives us not simply his memoir but a prescription for all on living life to the fullest. It is the story of a young man, a 'little rough around the edges' but with a desire to make something of his life. McKenna's life lessons learned in his years in the Navy and laid bare in his candid prose will help readers steer their own steady course and make the necessary corrections for the ups and downs encountered in military or civilian life."

—**Rona Simmons**, author of *The Other Veterans of World War II: Stories from Behind the Front Lines* and *A Gathering of Men*

"The men and women who shape their lives around the craft of landing airplanes on pitching flight decks are a rare bunch indeed. Steve gives the reader a wonderfully intimate and surprisingly transparent view into the world of naval aviation. Steve's craft is not only that of flying carrier-based aircraft, but also of telling the story in a way that brings the reader into the moment. He faithfully conveys a sense of the sacrifice, discipline, and intensity with which naval aviation must be approached.

"Flying on and off carriers is exciting, rewarding, often treacherous, and never boring. It is intolerant of mediocrity. Steve's book conveys naval aviation for what it is—a crucible through which few men and women pass, and having passed, are better for it."

—**Curtis G. Phillips (Otis)**, Citation X Captain, Captain USN (Retired)

"It was not until I read *Fair Winds* that I developed a greater sense of the person Steve is and a full appreciation of the devotion he brought to the service of his country as a naval pilot in the years prior to our meeting. His biography is easily readable and profoundly candid, covering both landings and 'bolters' during his life and career. The intensity of Steve's experience and his devotion to duty are reflected in the strength of the friendships he formed in the service. Those friendships clearly endure and are merited."

—**George Curtis,** retired partner at Gibson Dunn and former co-director of enforcement at the US Securities and Exchange Commission

"The challenging and very dangerous Naval aviation skill of flying off and landing on an aircraft carrier and guiding aircraft through that harrowing aerial maneuver falls to a very limited number of people. The number is very small because so few people could ever begin to qualify for such a difficult role. Steve McKenna pursued that long and arduous path, and he writes a balanced and engaging account of his experiences in *Fair Winds, Following Seas, and a Few Bolters.* It is a Navy story that needs to be told, and Steve does it with skill and an obvious and deserved pride in the U.S. Navy and of the time he spent in that service.

"No one could live such harrowing life experiences without some concluding observations and life lessons, and Steve McKenna does not fail to do so. He provides hard won insights into human nature and wisdom gleaned from his years of flying and guiding aircraft under the most trying conditions. This book rates a 'Bravo Zulu' and needs to be read by military folks of all ages, stripes, and backgrounds."

—**Col. Joseph R. Tedeschi**, US Army (Retired), author of *A Rock in the Clouds A Life Revisited*

"When my high school friend Steve reached out to me for advice on marketing a new book, I did not know what to expect. What I found was a good friend and a book that taught me a lot about what it takes to serve and protect our great country and its many liberties. Read along as Steve takes you through an honest, funny, and at times frightening tale that highlights the hard work and unflagging determination it takes to become and serve as a naval aviator."

—**Lisa Jochim**, author and publisher

"'Life is a cruel teacher; it gives the test first then teaches the lesson.' With simple honesty and engaging prose, Steve's book reminds us of the success possible when one builds upon those lessons."

—**David Busse (Busman)**, Commander USN (Retired)

"Life in naval aviation, particularly carrier naval aviation, is challenging, dangerous, rewarding, character building and, more often than not, extremely fun. Steve's description of that life was spot on and brought back many fond and sometimes scary memories of my twenty-six years in naval aviation as a member of the E-2C Hawkeye community. Having served several years with Steve, he was one of the best pilots and instructors I had the pleasure of flying with. The experiences and life lessons that you learn while serving in the military, whether for four, eight or thirty years form the person you are post military life, and the reader can see how that played out in Steve's successful, post-Navy career as an attorney."

—**Jim McHugh**, Captain USN (Retired)

"Fascinating, educational, and a fun read. McKenna pulls the veil on naval aviation while offering a candid and uplifting call for us to be the best humans we can be."

—**Galen D. Peterson**, author of *Strike Hard and Expect No Mercy: A Tank Platoon Leader in Iraq*

"The courage of honesty, like the kind written in these pages, is an inspiration which never wanes. Reading Clyde's stories and musings evoked fond feelings for lifetime buds, and shipmates we didn't get to bring home. His words put the 'who' in those of us who were 14-week wonders, climbing that mountain and then earning a set of the coveted golden wings. Rising from humble beginnings, we accepted the grind associated with 'the pursuit of happiness,' because we were taught that nothing of value is free.

"Clyde and I being born the same day in 1962 often referred to ourselves as brothers of different mothers, Brother thanks for telling the story, 'It's a good Story,' and thanks for leaving in the fun parts! As I recall, that first exhilarating trap and cat shot were life changing! In that moment, *we* were all unlimited."

—**Spike Long**, Captain USN (Retired)

"There is no greater legacy than a military memoir; it echoes generations and breaks the military-civilian divide. McKenna has written a vivid, crystal clear account that holds no punches: a dynamic life as a naval aviator."

—**Aaron Michael Grant**, US Marine Staff NCO, award-winning author of *Taking Baghdad: Victory in Iraq with the US Marines*

"From ward rooms to ready rooms, training flights to combat sorties, Steve McKenna gives you an exciting look into the lives of the seldom explored E2-C Hawkeye crews. Only someone who has lived the life of a carrier based pilot can give you insight like this. Steve is that writer. He's 'been there and done that' in spades. A great read for sailors and non-sailors alike."

—**Clay E. Novak**, Lt.Col. US Army (Retired), author of *Keep Moving, Keep Shooting*

Fair Winds, Following Seas, and a Few Bolters

by Stephen C. McKenna

© Copyright 2022 Stephen C. McKenna

ISBN 978-1-64663-850-5

Published by

◂ köehlerbooks™

3705 Shore Drive
Virginia Beach, VA 23455
800-435-4811
www.koehlerbooks.com

FAIR WINDS, FOLLOWING SEAS,

and a Few Bolters

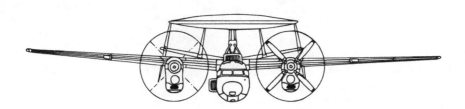

Stephen C. McKenna

VIRGINIA BEACH
CAPE CHARLES

This book is dedicated to those who made the ultimate sacrifice defending the country they loved, as well as those who cherish the liberty they died to protect.

TABLE OF CONTENTS

AVIATORS ARE A RARE AND strange breed. The men and women who ply their craft catapulting off and crashing back onto aircraft carriers are rarer and stranger still.

My years in the Navy, 1985–1994, flying amidst this flock with Spike, Reif, Otis, and others, spanned the successful ends of the Cold War and the First Gulf War. Following fleet duty, I instructed the next batch of E-2C Hawkeye pilots.

But first, a bit of backstory.

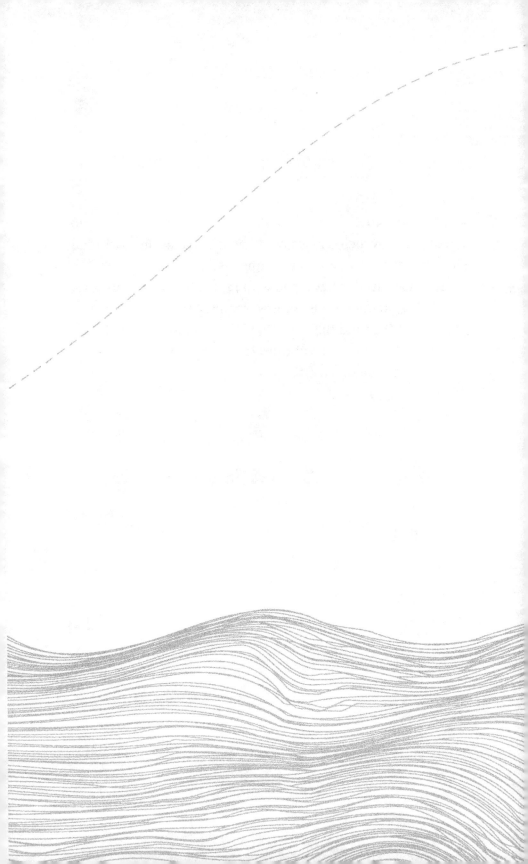

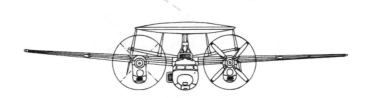

SECTION I:
A BIT OF BACKSTORY

CHAPTER 1

THE EARLY YEARS

I CAME INTO THE WORLD, breech, in March of 1962. Since then, I have tended to dive into life headfirst. I was the second child to my mother, Sally, and the first to my father Chuck.

The pictures I have of young Sarah Jane Morgan depict a pretty, pig-tailed girl with a thoughtful and mischievous look in her eye. Sally's mother once reprimanded her for lying on her stomach in the damp grass and touching tongues with a garter snake. Pictures of the young James Charles McKenna show a trim, determined young man. Sally and Chuck were classmates at the local public school where both my grandmothers, Margaret McKenna and Pauline Morgan, taught elementary.

Chuck's dad, my Grandpa Jim, worked as the head cook ("Don't call me a damn chef!") at the Detroit House of Corrections, the local prison we all called DeHoCo. Sally's dad, whom we called Poppa, killed himself with a shotgun blast to the chest when I was four. Sally's first husband and the father of my sister Kathy also died tragically and too young, of complications following surgery to repair a congenital ulcer, shortly after she was born.

Chuck had enlisted in the Marines to protest his occasional high-school sweetheart's first marriage, but the two reunited at the University of Michigan. They got married and Sally bore me shortly before graduating.

After graduation, Chuck got a job with Lockheed Aerospace

in California and we moved to Sausalito. Chuck thought nothing of renting a small plane and flying his infant son to their new home on the West Coast shortly after completing his first solo flight and earning his pilot's license. Sally and Kathy drove west with their meager belongings.

My initial stay in California was short-lived. Chuck got a job in Huntington, West Virginia, where Sally gave birth to my sister Sarah in June of 1965. The McKennas did not last long in West Virginia either. Before I started kindergarten, we moved to my parents' hometown of Plymouth, Michigan, and Chuck launched a thirty-year career with the Ford Motor Company at its world headquarters in Dearborn. He had a secretary and worked in an office housed in an enormous steel and glass building on the Ford campus. I found it quite impressive. My dad was chasing better jobs for those first three moves, the rest were mostly on my mother—and then on me and the Navy. To date, I have lived in the great states of Michigan (twice), California (three times), West Virginia, Georgia, Florida (twice), Texas (twice), and Colorado.

While growing up however, Plymouth, Michigan served as our mooring point. We stayed there while I attended kindergarten through third grade, living in a perfectly adequate home in a perfectly respectable middle-class subdivision. I got into my first fight in Plymouth.

Like most third graders, my parents encouraged me to learn to play an instrument. That is, Mom told me, "You're going to learn to play an instrument, Steve. Pick one." I chose the trombone. Band practice took place at school and I rode the bus. That meant I not only carried my *Johnny Quest* lunchbox and schoolbooks back and forth every day, I also carried my trombone. As you might imagine, an eight-year-old wisp of a boy juggling his lunchbox, books, and trombone case while boarding and disembarking a bright yellow school bus could be a sight to see.

One day, a particularly sinister fellow third grader decided to start calling me "Tromboner." *Ahh, the rapier-like wit of young boys.* This teasing, which I found humiliating, persisted on bus rides both to and from school for a few days before I could not take it anymore. Begging him to "please stop," with tears welling up in my eyes proved an abject failure, only heightening the ridicule—so I resolved to call the bully out.

The next morning, upon trundling up to the bus stop, I was greeted with a sneering:

"Look who's here, it's *Tromboner.*"

In response I declared, loudly and publicly: "That's enough. You and I are fighting after school."

That silenced both my tormentor and the crowd. Hushed whispers permeated the bus during the short ride to school.

It was not quite Gary Cooper in *High Noon*, but at three thirty on a crisp spring afternoon, a circle of schoolmates formed around us at the neighborhood bus stop. An older boy started chanting "fight, fight, fight," and a chorus of classmates chimed in on cue. My heart raced and my clenched fists quivered.

I do not recall who threw the first punch; it may have been me. I threw the last. I did not hurt the other boy badly, but I gave him a bloody nose, ending the fight. He got in a blow or two as well, but I do not really remember that. What I do remember is how I felt after standing up for myself. I had done nothing to antagonize him, yet he took it upon himself to tease me relentlessly, embarrassing me in front of a group of kids I desperately wanted as friends. I was shy and did not make friends easily. But now I had taken on a bully. It felt great. And while I have been called many things since, some good and some bad, Tromboner left the lexicon entirely. That is until I made the mistake of telling this story to my precocious daughter, who adopted the moniker immediately. *Tromboner* still shows up on her cell phone when I call.

Mom and Dad did not take much interest in the incident. They both asked if I was all right and whether I had hurt the other boy.

Upon assuring themselves that neither of us was much worse for the wear, that was the end of that. From this altercation I learned that there is absolutely nothing wrong with standing up for yourself if someone unjustly attacks you.

Jesus asks us to "turn the other cheek," and that is wise counsel. But once you have been slapped on both cheeks and are expecting another round, it is time for a change of strategy. In my view, society is mistaken to think it abnormal for young boys and girls to tease each other or get into fights. Conflict is a part of life that is not going away. The sooner we learn to deal with it, the better. Please do not misunderstand, I do not condone bullying, or violence—other than as a last resort. But to deny that life involves conflict, or to ignore it in a vain hope that it will go away, only exacerbates it.

My Tromboner victory gave me some self-confidence, and a modicum of standing on the playground. But one day not long after the fight, another boy said something to infuriate me. I do not remember what, but whatever it was, it led me to throw a rock at him while he hung from the jungle gym. I missed, but a firm grip at the back of my collar signaled instantly that I was in trouble.

Mr. Andreas dragged me into the gymnasium and then the equipment room. No explanation was necessary or given. "Bend over and grab your ankles," he ordered. I obeyed. Nervously glancing back between my spread legs, I glimpsed the orange plastic hockey stick Mr. Andreas' muscular, dark-haired forearm pulled from an equipment bin. Three crisp slap shots pummeled my behind. Gordy Howe would have been proud. I found the pain, and even more so the embarrassment, of being punished in this way excruciating. But the lesson endures. You do not resort to violence when someone merely offends you. Escalation may be necessary to protect against the actions of others, but not their words. "Sticks and stones may break my bones, but words will never hurt me," is a childhood ditty sadly sacrificed on the altar of political correctness.

You may sense an inconsistency here because the Tromboner fight was about resorting to violence because of name calling. The difference I see is that the verbal assault continued for days and my pleas to stop only resulted in more teasing. My choices were to either continue trying to ignore the bully or take the next step after verbal persuasion failed. I believe I was justified because the other boy was not just thinking and saying I was a geek for carrying around a trombone, he was incessantly harassing me about it. Thus, my antagonist had crossed the line between speech and action.

On the other hand, I was not justified in throwing the rock. First, I do not even remember what the other boy said to set me off, so it could not have been that important. Second, I skipped right past confronting my adversary face-to-face and escalated to throwing a rock that could do a lot more damage than he had inflicted, or than I could impart with my eight-year-old fists.

CHAPTER 2

GROWING UP IN RURAL MICHIGAN

AFTER THIRD GRADE, MY PARENTS were ready for a move. Some of my fondest memories are of the farm we lived on in Gregory, Michigan for the next three-and-a-half years. Mom and Dad rented a hundred-year-old house on 365 acres off Dutton Road, forty miles west of Plymouth. A group of doctors owned the property as a tax shelter. The Taylors, our closest neighbors, operated a dairy farm on the other side of the dirt road. They milked the hundred Holstein cows that produced their livelihood early every morning and every afternoon, rain or shine, sleet or snow. They also sowed and reaped the wheat and hay grown on our acreage. It was arduous work. I can still picture the scarred knuckles swollen with arthritis on Grandpa Taylor's weathered hands.

My sisters and I loved to play at the Taylors' and help with the afternoon milking, which involved attaching a milking harness to the cows' teats to extract the milk. Milk straight from a cow is warm (whatever a cow's body temperature is) and sweet. It was great fun to grab a bloated teat in your hand and squirt the milk into your mouth, a sister's, or the grateful mouths of the many feral cats scurrying around the Taylor's barn.

Mom and Dad bought an old quarter horse and her colt shortly after moving in. My sisters and I watched the dirt road in excited anticipation all day until, finally, a battered Ford F-100 stirred up dust towing a horse trailer into the driveway. Once out of the trailer, Mom let Kathy and me each take a lead line and guide the horses into their stall in the barn. Dad named the mare the "Dutton Dame." We called her DD. We named DD's feisty colt Slim. Shortly after the truck and trailer departed, Dr. Floyd Lundquist, a large-animal veterinarian straight out of *All Creatures Great and Small*, arrived. He examined the horses and asked Dad if he knew that DD was blind. He had not. Dad suggested we call the ranch where we bought her and see about taking her back but was quickly overruled; DD and Slim were now family members.

My father enlisted me, his younger brother Pat, and Grandpa Jim, to build a horse corral behind the barn. It was the first of many projects we undertook on the farm. We spent two weeks of hot, humid summer days soaking fence posts in creosote and planting them in the holes we dug with a posthole digger. At age nine, I helped my dad hold down Slim while watching Dr. Lundquist castrate him. Before the castration, Slim was a handful. At least once a week, we would get home from school and spend the chilly fall afternoon tracking him down after he had broken through the electric fence, again, to gallop through the neighboring fields. Getting a rope around his neck was never easy.

Primary responsibility for the horses fell to Kathy, though all three of us mucked the stalls. We made games of the work, with Kathy ordering me around and me passing down the orders to six-year-old Sarah, as siblings do. In addition to the horses, Sarah raised chickens and I bought two young bulls using my savings from the five-dollar bills in nine years of birthday and Christmas cards and earnings from working around the farm. We named my first entrepreneurial effort Frick and Frack. The plan was to feed and tend to them for a year before selling them for slaughter.

One wet autumn day, I walked down a dirt path between Frick and Frack, holding a lead line attached to their halters in each hand. A large, mottled-gray rat snake slithered across the muddy path and spooked the young bulls. Frick bolted forward, followed by Frack. I bounced between them, clinging to the lead lines. After finally letting go, I stood up, spit out the mud, and tracked down my charges.

Frack got sick that winter. I spent the night with him in the stall of a freezing barn doing what I could after the vet gave him a shot and a dire prognosis. He died shortly before dawn. Frack dying made me angry. I viewed it as a failure on my part but projected the blame onto him for dying. My parents understood that I had done my best, though, faithfully getting up before sunrise on frigid winter mornings to feed them and break the ice in the horse trough that formed overnight. (What a miserable task. The ice would often be two inches thick, requiring a half dozen hard whacks with an axe handle to break through. And when it did, the trough typically responded to the intrusion with a douse of freezing water.)

Mom and Dad replaced Frack with Blitz, who fattened up nicely before we sold the bulls in the spring. Thanks to my parents covering the loss of Frack, my efforts yielded a tidy profit. It made me a little sad to sell them to slaughter. But that was always the plan, and I love a good steak.

I got Brandy, an Appaloosa, after fourth grade. She stood sixteen hands tall at the withers. You measure horses in hands (four inches) and the withers are the top of the forelegs. Brandy was mean, and smart. Once while Brandy galloped through the back fields—me hanging onto the saddle horn for dear life, feet flapping wildly in the stirrups—she spied a branch hanging horizontally from a tree about eighteen hands off the ground. That filly sped up, ducked her head, and let that branch hit me square in the stomach to free herself of my bothersome presence. Another trick Brandy liked was to rub against the pine planks of the corral while you were riding, knowing that it hurt your leg a lot more than it hurt her. You did not wear shorts when riding Brandy in the corral.

I won my first trophy on Brandy. Kathy and I participated in a 4H (Head, Heart, Hands, and Health) horse camp that summer. Kathy rode with skill. I survived. Brandy liked to buck. She threw me from the saddle to land sprawling in the dirt multiple times that week. But by the end I had gotten her mostly under control. They awarded me the "Most Improved" trophy. I am still proud of that trophy, though I lost it decades ago.

Today, I prefer motorcycles to horses, although horses are great too. Motorcycles are inexpensive compared to a horse, or car—to purchase, maintain, and operate—fun to ride and work on (*Zen and the Art of Motorcycle Maintenance* is a terrific book), and do not buck you off, smash you into branches, or embed splinters through your J.C. Penny jeans and into your leg by scraping against the corral.

We moved off the farm after sixth grade when the doctor group wanted to sell. My parents could not afford the farm, so they bought, with the help of the bank, another ancient farmhouse on three-and-a-half acres on Hanford Road in Canton, Michigan. We lived in the Hanford house while I attended Plymouth Middle School and Plymouth Canton High School.

For the six years I lived on Hanford Road, the family shared a single shower, located over a bathtub in the upstairs bathroom. Dad got up and out during the week to make the long commute to Dearborn before the rest of us awoke. So, I shared the bathroom with my mom and two sisters in the morning. I learned to get in and out of a shower in record time. A delightful book I read as a kid was *Cheaper by the Dozen*, about an efficiency expert with twelve children. Ever since, I have critically examined almost everything to determine how to do it most efficiently. I can be a bit obsessive and compulsive—or as I prefer to frame it: meticulous.

CHAPTER 3

THE ROAD TO THE NAVY

MY HIGH-SCHOOL GUIDANCE COUNSELOR, NOTING my 3.9 GPA, varsity letters in swimming, and varied job history (I had held a paying job of one sort or another since age eleven), assumed I would matriculate at the University of Michigan. That is what top students at my high school did. I had other ideas. I had spent my entire life in Michigan, outside of a few years in California and West Virginia that were not in my memory bank. I wanted to try something else. Michigan is a beautiful state, but like most of the Midwest, the winters are cold, gray, and seemingly endless. Duke University, in North Carolina, was the farthest north I applied. I also applied to Stanford, Rice, the University of Virginia, and Georgia Tech. The admissions offices made the decision of where to go easy; only Georgia Tech accepted me.

In hindsight, I view it as a blessing. I visited all five schools on a trip with my dad and fell in love with the red tile roofs and palm trees on the campus Leland and Jane Stanford founded in Palo Alto, California in 1885, the same year Georgia Tech was founded. But the price tag was formidable, even in 1980. I did not really think about it at the time, but I imagine my life would have been much different had I attended Stanford, Duke, or UVA. I would have graduated saddled with an immense amount of debt and likely would have taken the highest paying job available to start paying it off. I doubt I would have joined the Navy.

I studied aerospace engineering at the Georgia Institute of Technology in Atlanta. My mom made me pick a major and it was first on the list. I earned mediocre grades, at best, but I learned a lot and had a lot of fun. My fraternity brothers at the Gamma Psi Chapter of Delta Tau Delta elected me president for my fourth year. As president, I presided at chapter meetings. I also oversaw the budget, run by the treasurer, and made sure the social chairman did not go too crazy with what he paid for the bands hired for parties. Otherwise, my main responsibilities were dealing with the interfraternity council and the police (usually campus, but occasionally Atlanta) when things got out of hand. Ordinarily, if you told the police that you would tone things down and then did, the encounter ended uneventfully. Other times, like when Jim and Fitz decided to burn their flea-infested sofa on the front lawn, the explanation proved more of a challenge.

As I began my last quarter at Georgia Tech in the unusually cold and occasionally snowy January of 1985, I had no idea what to do after graduation. I had worked as an engineer for Delta Airlines at the Atlanta Hartsfield International Airport every other quarter for the past three-and-a-half years in Tech's co-operative program. This, along with a few other odd jobs, supplemented the student loans I used to pay for school. I found the work at Delta dull and did not want to start an engineering career.

Scott Bailey and I spent the previous summer touring the continental United States on motorcycles. We spent three months traversing the United States from Georgia to Miami, Florida and then across to California, up to Washington, across to Maine, and back home to Atlanta. It was a memorable adventure, but I was still not ready for a desk job—not that there were any enticing offers. Several friends got good jobs with established engineering firms like Martin Marietta, Boeing, Grumman, and others. Barry Brady, a fraternity brother and frequent racquetball opponent, went to work for a computer software firm founded in Albuquerque in 1975 by Paul Allen and Bill Gates. Microsoft developed the MS-DOS operating system for personal computers. After an initial public offering in 1986, it went on to some success. Barry bought a sailboat not long after the IPO and toured the world by water with his wife. Jobs like that sounded interesting and financially rewarding but were not being offered to students with a 2.6 overall GPA.

Shortly before my mid-life crisis at age twenty-two, I watched the movie *An Officer and a Gentleman*, starring Richard Gere, Debra Winger, and Lou Gossett, Jr. It told the story of a young man who was a little rough around the edges and wanted to make something of his life. He signed up for the Navy's Aviation Officer Candidate School (AOCS) in Pensacola, Florida. If you could survive the school, the Navy would make you an officer and teach you to fly jets. Feeling boundless and intrigued, I walked into a recruiting office.

My parents raised my sisters and me to be patriotic citizens and to appreciate the freedoms inherent in living in the United States of America. Further, as a first grader, I participated in atomic attack drills during the early stages of the Cold War, hiding with the other students under our desks. *Like that was going to help.* I thought: *What better way to serve the country I love than to have it pay me to fly jets off aircraft carriers to defend it?* I passed the tests and the Navy accepted me into the program. Raising my right hand, I solemnly swore an oath:

> To support and defend the Constitution of the United States against all enemies, foreign and domestic; that I will bear true faith and allegiance to the same; and I will obey the orders of the President of the United States and the orders of the officers appointed over me, according to regulations and the Uniform Code of Military Justice. So help me God.

With a plan in place, I did not put much effort into my final quarter of studies. Although I did work hard on the design project where my team spent two quarters designing a business jet with forward swept wings. I managed to get a C in that course, to go along with a C in Analysis of Aircraft Structures, Ds in Vibration and Flutter and Mechanical Vibrations, which I had dropped in the fall to avoid an F, and a Satisfactory in Investments. That 1.5 GPA brought my overall down to a 2.5. But I graduated with a Bachelor of Science degree in aerospace engineering from one of the top engineering schools in the world. I anxiously anticipated what came next.

The Navy sent me orders to report to Naval Air Station (NAS) Pensacola, the *Cradle of Naval Aviation,* for AOCS at noon on Sunday, July 14, 1985. My college roommate and the fraternity social chairman the year I was president, Charles Bowen, his father, and his uncle were competing in a deep-sea fishing tournament a few days before I was due to report and invited me along. We departed Panama City on their fifty-five-foot Hatteras, *The Great Escape*, early Thursday morning to pursue marlin and other trophy fish in the Gulf of Mexico. A squall arose out of the west midday on Friday. It gradually turned into a violent storm, making fishing impossible. Instead, we hunkered down in the cabin, played cards, drank, and ate while *The Great Escape* rose, fell, rocked, and swayed in a turbulent gulf.

I have always enjoyed the rise and fall of a boat on the water, even in rough seas. The constancy of the motion is comforting. As with most things in life, a large body of water is always moving and changing. Resisting this inherent fluidity, while required from time to time, can be hazardous. Whether a small boat on a vast ocean, or an individual amongst nearly eight billion others on the planet, the best you can do is steer a steady course, making corrections to account for the ups and downs you encounter along the way.

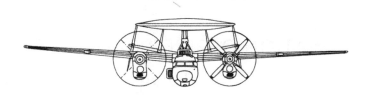

SECTION II:
BECOMING AN OFFICER AND LEARNING TO FLY

CHAPTER 4

AVIATION OFFICER CANDIDATE SCHOOL

I ARRIVED AT NAS PENSACOLA, at the western end of the Florida panhandle, a little later than I planned on Sunday. I overslept a bit after a nice dinner on Saturday with the Bowens and underestimated the length of the ride from Panama City to Pensacola. I pulled up to the guard station at the gates of the naval air station at a quarter to noon, when I was due to report, parked, walked into the building, and announced:

"I'm here for AOCS."

"Orders," commanded a uniformed guard with a chevron and stripes on his sleeve that meant nothing to me, extending a white gloved hand.

I presented my orders and, after examining them, the guard gave me convoluted directions to Battalion I headquarters. Exiting the guard shack, those directions quickly evaporated in the swirl of thoughts careening through my head. I remounted my black Honda Sabre 750 motorcycle and rode into an array of tidy brick buildings, Quonset huts, and manicured lawns trimmed with decorative rocks painted white. Maneuvering around aviation officer candidate classes marching smartly in formation to some destination or another, I traversed the base, trying to get my bearings.

Upon locating the imposing red brick building that served

as Battalion I headquarters. I quickly parked my bike in the closest available parking space. Walking past a tall white flagpole flying an enormous American flag, I approached a set of stone steps, atop which a heavy oak door stood between me and my future. With some serious trepidation, I pulled open the door, wondering: *What have I gotten myself into this time?*

Upon entering, three trim young men with buzz cuts and wearing khaki uniforms screamed at me to "stand at attention, heels four inches from the bulkhead, eyes front!" Amidst being berated for being late (I was not, I arrived at noon sharp but had not yet learned: "if you're not early, you're late") and ordered to report to my barracks immediately, I managed to ask where I should park my motorcycle. The young men were not pleased with this interruption in the indoctrination. But, to their credit, realized they could not just leave a motorcycle parked out front in a visitor's spot for the next fourteen weeks. They gave me three minutes to put my bike in a long-term parking lot and "hightail" my ass back to the battalion.

Checking into the barracks, I greeted fellow candidates sitting cross-legged on their racks studying arcane military information that would soon be committed to memory. We engaged in some small talk but were mostly lost in our own thoughts, keenly aware that whatever we had been through before, this was different.

At 0555 on Monday, the base speakers, mounted on towering white poles outside the barracks, blared: "Reveille, reveille, reveille. All hands heave to and trice up. Morning PT will go down in five minutes."

After groggily pulling on our sneakers and making a trip to the head (bathroom), we embarked on a five-mile run along the seawall led by a senior candidate. Following a quick shower and breakfast, another senior candidate marched us to the Naval Aerospace Medical Institute (NAMI), which performed a merciless medical culling.

Dozens of candidates fell victim to the *NAMI whammy*. The NAMI physical was thorough, to say the least. It took all day, as white-cloaked technicians poked and prodded us in places I had never been prodded or poked. The medical staff deemed candidates medically unfit for heart murmurs, flat feet, and, most often, lack of twenty-twenty vision. Who knew the fine line between sailor and civilian could be delineated by the height of one's arch?

Despite the staff's poking resulting in NAMI deeming me physically qualified, I found all of it quite overwhelming. Scores of young men from across America came to Pensacola to pursue a dream, and in just one day, NAMI quashed that dream with a test that revealed a physical anomaly they never knew they had.

Several candidates washed out as pilots due to lack of twenty-twenty vision but were otherwise qualified. They could either continue with the program toward the goal of becoming a naval flight officer (NFO) or aviation maintenance duty officer (AMDO), equally important roles, or drop on request (DOR) and go home. Many began the pursuit to become an NFO or AMDO, but many others had their hearts set on being a pilot. Those who took that setback in stride and continued to pursue their goal to serve in their best capacity earned my utmost respect. And those that chose to quit at that point, or any other throughout AOCS and flight school, were no lesser in my view for making that choice. The path we had chosen was clearly not meant for everyone.

Class 33-85 met our drill instructor (DI) on Tuesday morning. On Monday, the battalion officers (senior candidates in their last week) warned us to fall out when called at 0500 within ten seconds or we'd "have hell to pay." My classmates and I slept nervously in the ill-fitting green trousers and T-shirts presented to us on Sunday upon assignment to the battalion, but to no avail. We ended up paying hell, with interest.

Gunnery Sergeant (Gy.Sgt.) Crenshaw, United States Marine Corps, non-commissioned officer in charge (NCOIC), as he was wont to be called, made an impression. A tall man at about six feet, four inches, Gy.Sgt. Crenshaw had a deep, commanding voice, and at least forty pounds of lean, sinewy muscle on me. He remains the scariest individual I have ever met.

Gy.Sgt. Crenshaw roused us by flinging a galvanized steel trash can into the concrete walls and off the tile floor of the barracks hallway, bellowing: "Fall out, you maggots." By taking two minutes instead of ten seconds to fall out, my classmates and I provided the sergeant with ample motivation to teach us what PT (physical training) meant to a Marine DI.

The AOCS DIs were also a rare breed. Unlike the other service branches, the Marines did not offer noncombat positions. Every Marine was first a fighter, a weapon of destruction encased in flesh and fueled by blood. And the DIs were some of the finest fighters in the Marines, ranking them amongst the fiercest warriors in the world. Each was heavily decorated. And when Gy.Sgt. Crenshaw or another DI would lean into you—the broad brim of their campaign hat pressing into your forehead as you stared down into a chest full of ribbons—for a dressing down over a smudged belt buckle or a crooked *gig line* it was terrifying. But without their terror, they would never have been great teachers.

A gig line is the vertical line from the button line of your shirt down through your belt buckle and the zipper line of your trousers. It really does look sloppy if they are misaligned. Gy.Sgt. Crenshaw taught us that you do not use a new razor blade to shave for an inspection, or a date—too easy to nick yourself and end up with a wad of toilet paper on your face to staunch the bleeding.

But the most important thing Gy.Sgt. Crenshaw and the other DIs taught us fledgling officers and aviators was a sense of the mental and physical toughness within each of us. While double-timing (jogging) through the sweltering heat of Pensacola in July and August, carrying an M-1 rifle and thinking there was no way you could go another hundred yards, let alone the mile and a half remaining, you would dig deep and find a hidden reserve of will that kept you going. A lot of that came from not wanting to let your DI down. As much as you hated them at times—for brutal PT or cancelling a meal for the entire class because the removal of our *chrome dome* helmets was not done in unison before marching into chow—you also respected them deeply.

It boggles the mind to consider their orders: take a group of cocky young men, weed out the ones that are not going to make it, and then mold the remainder into a cohesive group willing to fight to the death to protect each other, their families, and their country. The success of the incredible DIs that molded us was no small accomplishment.

Following forty-five minutes of PT, administered by the DI who would both terrorize and mentor us over the next fourteen weeks, we quickly doffed our PT gear and donned our green trousers and T-shirts, adding a chrome helmet to complete the ensemble. We then embarked on a disorderly march to the mess hall for breakfast. Assembled at the entrance, Gy.Sgt. Crenshaw instructed us on proper chow line procedures:

"Line up, line up, you worthless maggots! Stand at attention! All right, on my command you will all reach up and grab your helmet with your right hand, remove them in unison, and announce: 'Class 33-85 marching into chow.'"

His baritone voice then barked out an order that would haunt us every day, three times a day, for the rest of our first week, appropriately called *poopy week*: "Reach up and grab 'em."

Our first attempt was an unmitigated disaster. Hands slapped into chrome helmets at erratic intervals. One candidate managed to drop his helmet into the dirt and Gy.Sgt. Crenshaw let him, and the rest of us, have it. The next few attempts were not much better. Finally, we got close enough that Gy.Sgt. Crenshaw allowed us to enter the mess hall.

"Stand at attention, grab a tray, and march through the line—

eyes front!" he commanded. As we did our best to comply, Gy.Sgt. Crenshaw walked up to the candidate in front of me, leaned in, and in a quiet tone that was more intimidating than his bellow warned:

"You'd better hold that tray level, boy. Keep those elbows bent at ninety degrees. And don't you eyeball me."

After instruction on the proper way to take your seat and location for silverware, napkins, and glasses, we devoured a bland breakfast of runny eggs, dry toast, and white milk or water. Following chow, Gy.Sgt. Crenshaw turned us over to a senior candidate who marched us to the barber shop. As the clippers crisscrossed my scalp and my shoulder-length locks fell to the floor, I metamorphosized, shedding one exterior and existence and developing another.

Bald, we marched to the uniform shop to get outfitted with uniforms and PT gear. As we waited our turn to collect our new wardrobe, the senior candidate ordered us to "mill about smartly." We improvised.

The Navy made us pay for the uniforms, but generously took it out of our upcoming paycheck rather than making us pay on the spot. It also promised to reimburse us if we made it through the school. The uniforms cost me that entire first paycheck, an irony I chuckled at bitterly. Then again, I had nothing else to spend that money on. I had enough for stationery and stamps, and it would be weeks before our class could go off base and blow our meager paychecks on dinner and drinks at Trader Jon's or shooting pool at the Flora-Bama.

One of the first things we learned at AOCS was how to approach the DI's office. You approached the entrance with your inboard shoulder exactly four inches from the bulkhead, stopping and standing at attention just shy of the opening. With your inboard hand you announced your presence by smacking the palm against the bulkhead three times. Upon hearing "enter," you took one step forward with your outboard leg, brought your heels together at a forty-five-degree angle, and executed a crisp right (or left) face, such that you were standing at attention in the doorway. You were to stare straight ahead until given permission to speak, upon which you stated your business.

Knock timidly, falter in executing the right (or left) face, or heaven forbid, look directly at the DI and hear "Don't you eyeball me boy!" and the DI doled out punishment. Usually it was twenty pushups, up downs, or leg lifts—legs held aloft while your abdominal muscles screamed until the DI gave you permission to lower them for a few seconds before commanding "legs up" again.

Occasionally, the DI ordered you to grab the tailhook that stood in the corner of the office and hold it in front of you with outstretched arms. As sweat began running down your temples and your deltoids, triceps, and quadriceps started quivering, you did your best to hold the heavy hook aloft. No one could do so for more than a minute or two.

I never understood the half a dozen or so candidates who DORed over the next few days. They usually quit during PT. Gy. Sgt. Crenshaw would have us doing jumping jacks, leg lifts, or push-ups; insisting we had no business attempting to be officers. He would then pick out a weaker candidate to focus his attention on, with remarkable success. For me, once I made it through NAMI, had my head shaved, and spent all my earnings on uniforms, there was no way I was quitting. Plus, I figured out the game relatively quickly. You did not have to do the most push-ups or finish first in every five-mile run, you just could not do the least or finish last. My strategy to compete but also conserve energy, pay attention, and not draw attention to myself, proved successful in the early weeks of the program.

I have reproduced my first two letters home from AOCS below. AOCS did not grant phone privileges until your class passed its fourth week room, personnel, and locker inspections, making letters the only form of communication with the outside world. Going through my parents' files while settling their estate, I came across a manila folder with my letters home from AOCS and two, six-month Western Pacific cruises. The letters reflect much that had faded from memory over the years. AOCS started for me and my classmates on Sunday July 14, 1985, so I wrote the first letter, dated July 21, after one week, when our initial class of seventy was already down to twenty-seven.

UNITED STATES NAVAL AIR STATION
Pensacola, Florida

21 July 1985

Dear Family,

My all-expense-paid vacation in Florida has been everything the brochures said and more. I strolled into regiment Sunday at 1200 on the dot in shorts, T-shirt, and sunglasses. I was immediately ordered four inches from the bulkhead, stand straight, eyes to the front, given three minutes to get my gear and park my bike, and taken up to my room, where three other candidates were studying gouge (general orders of a sentry, chain of command, enlisted and officer insignia, etc.). We took a power test that afternoon (push-ups, sit-ups, and pull-ups). That was pretty easy and then went to a lecture by the CO, AOCS Capt. J.E. Goodman, after which two candidates DOR'd, a real inspiration.

Monday we all marched (badly) over to NAMI, the medical facility, and spent the day being tested, eyes, ears, teeth, heart, blood, urine, height, weight, and breath for all I know. Anyway, I was pronounced PQ (physically qualified) and quite happy about it. Eighteen candidates weren't (most pilots). That took all day Monday and we anxiously awaited our meeting with the DI (drill instructor).

Tuesday morning came as a shock. We had been warned to fall out quickly to make a good impression, under ten seconds considered quickly, so most of us slept in our green pants, T-shirt, and socks. We didn't all get out however, until almost 0502 and the DI, Gy.Sgt. Crenshaw, was furious for waiting. The next forty-five minutes were spent doing push-ups till we could do no more, switching to leg lifts till they were impossible, and then jumping jacks till the balls of our feet cried. Repeat, repeat. The whole time we were yelling at the top of our lungs how we would get motivated and would pay attention to detail.

We took a swimming test Tuesday too and lost four more candidates. Meals are totally regimented including placement of food, utensils, and glasses, walking, sitting, adjusting, and what we can eat and drink. Wednesday and Thursday were much the same, with some lectures interspersed. This was when candidates really started dropping like flies.

By Friday morning when we had our outpost RLP (room, locker, and personnel inspection), we were down to twenty-seven candidates from around seventy. There they PTed us and scattered our gear. Then we packed all our gear except breakables in our gear bag and fell out on line. Unfortunately, our room was one of the first inspected and we had to hold our gear bags straight-armed in front of us until the other candidates came out. Then we assembled and ran (stopped PT), ran, stop, with our bags to regiment, where we PTed with the bags some more.

I realize I've been telling you the bad for two pages here (that's how it started), but it's really not that bad. On Tuesday we bought all sorts of gear: four pair khaki pants, one white, shirts to match, three belts, three covers, two pair of shoes (white and black), raincoat, underwear, and insignia. Wednesday, we bought flight boots. The Navy supposedly gives us $500 to pay for all this when we graduate. The fact that I would owe them for what I've used, plus the fact they shaved our heads on Tuesday will surely keep me from DORing.

Battalion I is pretty nice, though. All the older candidates are nice and gouge us in on what we should know. We aren't actually in the battalion until after the rifle run tomorrow (Mon.). That's where we double time (run) two miles to where we pick up our M-1s and then double time back another two miles (150 yards of it thru soft sand). We just got some good news from our candidate officers. These are candidates in their fourteenth week who are atop their class and selected to help the other classes. They informed us that there is a female from G company running with us and the pace will be slower.

I've also met a lot of good people here. The mix is from all over the country, all schools, all majors. There are also several men from the service who were selected. They are twenty-seven to twenty-nine and have about eight years service average. I've gotten to be good friends with a few of them as well as "men" my own age. Things are looking up and should continue to do so. Hopefully, we'll get into our personal locker tonight and I can get a stamp to mail this. I'm really sorry to be away but I know you'll all get by without me. Love and miss you all.

Steve

Ultimately, eighteen of the original seventy graduated together. I wrote the second letter four days later.

UNITED STATES NAVAL AIR STATION
Pensacola, Florida

25 July 1985

Dear Family

I just got your wonderful letters and was delighted to hear that everything went well. Sorry I missed the wake.

Things have settled into somewhat of a routine here. Up at 0500 still and doing either calisthenics or running for around forty-five minutes. The day is divided into periods and I don't think they know what a free period is. For PT we're doing survival swimming and boxing and we're into two academic classes, Naval Organization, and Operations and Administration. The first test is tomorrow morning. We also have two periods of Drill with good ole Gy.Sgt. Crenshaw, USMC NCOIC. We're working with the rifles now. We didn't lose anyone on the rifle run, but a really fine candidate DORed today, so we're at thirty-two.

Dad, please start baking and send lots. I got some brownies from Martha's mom today and even though everybody only got a third of one, we were all grateful. Our diet is very strict. We haven't earned butter, salad dressing, juice, fruit, dessert, or anything sweet yet (Gy.Sgt.) and all we can drink is white milk or water, pretty bland. I've been looking forward to Sunday all week because then I can go in our two-block unsecured liberty radius and get ice cream (mountains).

We are allowed visitors Sunday from 1200-1600 on base and Martha might be coming by. I really hope so, as it would be nice to see someone from the real world with hair and nice legs and all. We're already getting ready for our four-week rifle inspection, which is the first time we can get secured (off-base privileges). I need a beer bad!

Well, I need to get back to the notes now, even though this stuff is really simple, mostly memorization, so I'll say so long. My best to everyone. Thanks for the letters.

Love,
Steve

The reference to missing the wake refers to a trying episode early in my Navy career. Shortly after starting the program, Gy.Sgt. Crenshaw drilled the class on a parade field under a scorching July sun. As he commanded *right shoulder—arms, present—arms, ready—arms,* and grew frustrated as we fumbled with our M-1 rifles, our class officer approached.

Lieutenant Loesline called out: "Candidate McKenna, come over here."

After looking to our DI and getting a "What the hell are you waiting for," I jogged over, stood at attention, and saluted—fearing I was in trouble.

"At ease candidate," Lt. Loesline said, saluting back.

I assumed the *parade rest* position. In less than a week, muscle memory was already taking hold to stand straight, shoulders back, with eyes front, as I moved my left foot to shoulder width and clasped my hands behind my back.

"I've got some sad news," he said softly, "your Grandma Margaret died in her sleep last night."

I blinked in shock as I took in the information. Sadness and loss swept through me. I spent sleepovers at Grandma Margaret and Grandpa Jim's both by myself and with my best friend Kevin Curran, who could not sleep at our house because he was allergic to our cat, Tilly. Grandma Margaret taught Kevin and me to play penny-ante poker and never went easy on us. When I was sick, she would let me sleep in her magnificent brass bed, feed me homemade chicken noodle soup, and stroke my forehead. She was a great lady.

Lt. Loesline explained that I had a choice. I could go home, attend the wake, and come back in a week or two to start over with a new class, or I could continue with Class 33-85. Having already started bonding with my classmates and made several friends, the idea of starting over was not appealing. I also feared I would not have the courage to come back.

I told Lt. Loesline, "Sir, I think I would like to stay with my class," and asked him to please give my condolences to my parents and family.

I regretted missing the funeral and wake, but never regretted the decision to stay at AOCS. I found myself on a path both exciting and challenging, and I very much wanted to continue testing myself.

A little over a month into the fourteen-week program, a third letter home reflected one of the brutalities of AOCS. I wrote about how five of my classmates were holding the class back. I was not the only one that felt this way; it was apparent to everyone, except possibly the five. I remember one ill-suited classmate well to this day. I will call him Chianti. Chianti had a swarthy complexion, and thick black eyebrows that unfortunately accentuated an already pronounced nervous twitch. Drilling was a challenge for all of us. But for Chianti, asking him to march in a straight line and do a crisp about face was like asking him to walk on his hands, blindfolded. And for whatever reason, he simply could not keep time with the rest of the platoon. These mistakes led Gy.Sgt. Crenshaw to continue drilling the entire class without respite or pity for hours.

Gunny Crenshaw would create dissention by having Chianti or another offending party call the cadence for all his classmates while watching them do calisthenics as punishment for his mistake. It worked. You felt bad for Chianti when the Gunny was screaming at him, but you also resented the fact that he kept screwing up. Five weeks into the program, I did not think Chianti and the other four were going to make it through. Quite frankly, I did not want them to because I did not trust them to have my back.

You need confidence, not only that your future fellow aviators and shipmates were willing to give their all for you, but also that their all was going to be enough to get the job done. I had no doubt Chianti would try his best. I just had little confidence in his best. This is harsh, but we were training for something important and potentially deadly. The Navy was putting us through this school, constantly evaluating us physically, mentally, and emotionally, because they needed to know they could trust us with a multi-million-dollar aircraft and the lives of our aircrew. I knew I did not want Chianti in control of a jet trying to get aboard a pitching aircraft carrier deck. Gy.Sgt. Crenshaw knew it too, which is why he rode him so hard that eventually he agreed to DOR. So did the other four.

I credited them all for how long they hung in there. And I felt badly that they put in six weeks only to be forced to give up their dream. They obviously wanted desperately to get through the school, but they were ill-suited, through no fault of their own.

On the bright side, once shed of some dead weight, Class 33-85 thrived. Gy.Sgt. Crenshaw, who had thankfully not paid much attention to me up to that point, made me the third squad leader. That meant I carried the guidon, a military standard or flag that hangs at the end of an eight-foot wooden pole and designates the unit. We started to look sharp marching around the base. Gy.Sgt. Crenshaw even offered an occasional "not too bad, boys" to go along with the criticism. I reflected on the marching candidate classes that captivated my attention while riding onto the base looking for Battalion I headquarters a half a dozen Sundays before. We were now captivating others with precision marching and rifle drills. It felt good, and our class really started to pull together.

AOCS classmates of note include Dean Patrick, from Hesperia, Michigan. Dean was a great guy and fantastic friend. I lived with him during primary flight training and served as best man when he married his lovely wife, Jamie. The Navy assigned Dean to fly the SH-3H Sea King helicopter out of Naval Air Station North Island in San Diego after flight school. Shortly after Jamie got pregnant, Dean failed to return from a training flight over the Pacific Ocean. They never found his aircraft or body. Dean's family came to California to comfort a devastated Jamie at the military funeral. Jamie bore their son, Drew, a few months later.

Another beloved classmate was David Lopez. Dave wore thick, black-framed glasses before they were stylish and was in the AMDO program. He was my greatest competition in the cross-country run and the obstacle course. I never did beat him, but by pushing each other, we turned in impressive times in both. Tragically, Dave died in a car accident a few years after AOCS.

Many other good friends helped me get through those fourteen weeks, including Wade King and Ernie Lashua. Wade had a warm, ready laugh, played golf in college, and dreamed of flying the A-7 Corsair II. Ernie enrolled in AOCS from the fleet, where he had served as a chief petty officer. I took up the pipe to smoke with Ernie and hear his sea stories.

Back at AOCS things continued to plod along. I was doing well in all three disciplines on which our instructors continually evaluated us—academics, military (marching, rifle drills, military knowledge, etc.), and physical training. Several classmates, however, continued to struggle, especially with the harder academic courses like Aerodynamics and Engines. Those of us with academics in hand did our best to help them along, but in a couple of cases otherwise strong candidates just could not pass the test. After two tries they went to G-Company, where they got another try. Most candidates assigned to G-Company eventually passed and were reassigned to a later class. Class 33-85 picked up several great classmates that way. If they could not pass, they were attrited—thanked for the effort and told to go home or wherever else they wanted, it just was not going to be the Navy. The obstacle course took out a few candidates as well.

Seemingly inspired by Spanish Inquisition-style torture devices, the Navy designed the AOCS obstacle course to include monkey bars, barbed wire to crawl under, ladders to run up, thin logs to run across, and a rope swing. Then there was the wall. Twelve feet high, rising out of the soft sand on which much of the course stood, it was feared by many, respected by all.

I no longer remember the times required to pass and to PT (earn highest points for achieving a set, faster time), but the course took around three-and-a-half minutes to PT and four to qualify. That does not sound like a long time, but as I discovered in boxing class, where Wade put my ass on the canvas with an uppercut after ducking my jab in the second round, three minutes can be an eternity. All the obstacles, even the easier ones, took a lot of effort to get over, under, or across.

The wall was different. You ran as fast as you could through the sand to build enough momentum to leap high and grasp the rope. It hurt when your body slammed into the hard oak planks. From there you had to brace your feet on the wall and pull yourself up to the top with the rope. Then, supporting your full weight with one arm you swung the other over the wall and hoisted yourself up and over. It was brutal. At a relatively tall six foot one, I had an advantage. How my shorter classmates managed to get over amazes me to this day.

The last few weeks of AOCS let you do the fun training you endured all the pain and suffering of the prior weeks to be allowed to try. The Dilbert Dunker involved strapping into a cockpit and riding it down rails until you splashed into a pool while wearing a helmet with a blackened visor. The goal was to release yourself from your four-point harness as the cockpit rolled over nose first into the pool and escape before drowning. Nobody drowned.

Nobody drowned in the helicopter escape either, but I took a couple of steel-toed flight boots to the mouth. This test simulated a helicopter crash at sea. There were twelve seats, a row of six on each side of the fuselage. Like the Dilbert Dunker, you strapped in while wearing a helmet with an opaque visor and instructors dropped the fuselage into the pool. You were taught to wait until the motion of the cage rolling upside down ceased before unstrapping with the other eleven submerged candidates and blindly groping your way toward the exit door. As candidates started to run out of oxygen, legs began to scissor and kick frantically. I endured two shots to the kisser before finding the door and then the surface of the pool.

Bay operations involved parasailing. But instead of gently landing back on the white sand beach or having the crew reel you back into the boat after a scenic tour over Pensacola Bay, instructors simply cut you free to parachute down into the water in boots and flight gear. The goal was similar to that of the Dunker, but here you had to get out of your harness and away from the parachute before it filled with water and sank, dragging you to the bottom of the bay with it. That never happened either. And if you or the chute started to sink, Navy divers stood by to save the day.

There was also the ejector seat shot that no doubt compressed a few vertebrae, a ride in the centrifuge to experience high g-forces, and a trip to 25,000 feet of altitude in the hypobaric chamber to experience hypoxia. It is truly commendable that our DIs and other instructors trained us as thoroughly and rigorously as they did with rarely an injury or incident.

We survived survival training. In late October, a bus took us to a forest, where we spent the day doing ground navigation with a map and compass. We identified which plants and bark were edible, and which were poisonous. There was no food other than some prickly pear cactus, which we were not hungry enough to do more than nibble on. We slept in tents in our clothes without sleeping bags and awoke after a fitful, shivering night to frozen canteens.

On day two, while exploring our environs further, we saw something rustling the brush. It turned out to be a small rattlesnake. Nonetheless, famished, we found a forked stick. Our instructor told us to be careful, because young rattlesnakes cannot moderate the amount of venom they release when striking—they give it all to you. Dave used the stick to pin the snake's head to the dirt. We separated the head and fangs from the snake with a survival knife, skinned the body, and used what little meat there was to make a thin gruel.

As AOCS neared its end, my fellow classmates and I eagerly anticipated the Regimental Ball. It promised to be a grand affair, with a formal dinner for our dates and ourselves followed by music and dancing. As future officers, the school required us to take an etiquette course to prepare for the dinner. We Philistines called it *knife and fork school*. The wife of Captain J. E. Goodman, the commanding officer (CO) of Naval Aviation Schools Command, taught the course.

Mrs. Goodman patiently explained the difference between

a salad and dinner fork, where the water and wine glasses were properly placed, and how to cut and eat a steak, one bite at a time, placing your knife and fork back on your plate after each so that you could engage in polite conversation without a mouthful of food. We horsed around a bit in the classes, but we also paid attention. We did not want to embarrass ourselves at the dinner and certainly did not want the CO's wife complaining about us. My college sweetheart, Martha Tuttle, accompanied me to the Regimental Ball. She looked lovely in a long, black dress that stood in striking contrast to my formal white uniform, called *chokers* due to the standing collar.

A fourth letter from AOCS I found among my parents' effects reflects these events.

UNITED STATES NAVAL AIR STATION
Pensacola, Florida

19 September 1985

Dear Family,

How's everything in the real world? I'm sorry I haven't written much lately but once again, we've been busy. However, we're almost done. We finished the last of our big three academic courses today with the Navigation final. Everyone in the class passed and I got a 100. We have a lot of guys down in Aero and they have an immediate retake next week, which they must pass or go to G-Company (holding company). Three guys go no matter what. That leaves just one test, the Naval Leadership final, after which we'll have a max. liberty policy!

Along with the test, we have out times for the obstacle and cross-country courses on Monday and

Tuesday. We get issued our flight gear (leather jackets and all) next week, too. From then on, it's mostly fun stuff like Bay Operations, First Aid, CPR, the dunker, helo pick-up, and survival (maybe not so fun).

The Regimental Ball is coming up next weekend and we are all very excited. Martha is coming and I'm really looking forward to seeing her. We dress out in our choker whites and the ladies all wear long dresses and there's a formal dinner and a dance and, and, and, it should be fun.

My duties as battalion first lieutenant have really been hard this past week. We are short two classes of workers because one class, 31, made honor class and doesn't have to do cleanup and the junior class, 41, is a week behind schedule and won't be in the battalion until Monday night. This leaves a lot of work for the rest of us and a lot of running around for me, but it gets done. This has given me good exposure and I'm hoping to make regimental commander (head honcho) during Candidate Officer Week (the week before graduation when the senior candidates run the regiment). I am also shooting for Distinguished Naval Graduate, which would get me a regular commission. All inspections are over now and we have kept our secured status. The inspections are the only things I haven't done too well on. My personal appearance is usually good and so is my knowledge, but I just can't justify spending hours folding socks and underwear and making my rack.

After graduation I will be staying in Pensacola and reporting to Whiting Field for primary training. Ground school for a month and then we start flying. I really can't wait. We start in T-34 Turbo Mentors (single-engine propeller) and then will fly the T-2 Buckeye (single-engine jet) and then the TA-4 (what the Blue Angels fly but a trainer version). Even though things are getting less frenzied, the more time you have, the more you wish you could spend it somewhere else. Oh well, only four more weeks.

Love,

Steve

Mom and Dad—Can't wait to see you at graduation. I promise a good time.

Things worked out well for me finishing AOCS. I ended up with top grades in all three disciplines and the designation of Distinguished Naval Graduate, which earned me a regular as opposed to a reserve commission. When the Navy honorably discharged me from service a little over eight years later, I had received no discernable benefit from the regular commission. In fact, the government respectfully declined to give me the $100,000 offered to resigning reserve officers in the post-Cold War service draw down. They also told me upon separation that as a regular Navy officer as opposed to a reservist, I could be recalled at any time according to "the needs of the Navy."

On the plus side, AOCS named me regimental commander and put me in charge of running both battalions for graduation week, with able assistance from the two battalion commanders and other selected candidate officers. At a pre-graduation ceremony in front of my parents, grandparents, Martha, and her parents, the instructors presented me with a sword for my accomplishments over the past fourteen weeks. Swordsmiths in Toledo, Spain forged and crafted the ceremonial weapon and my instructors had my name engraved on the blade. An instructor's wife told my mom that this only happened once or twice a year. To top it all off, as Regimental Commander I led the candidates from Battalions I and II onto the graduation parade field, assembled them into formation, and saluted the dais with my new sword in front of the crowd of proud parents and other guests. That may not have been worth $100,000—but then again, maybe?

Capt. Goodman read *A Navy Flyer's Creed* at the graduation ceremony:

A Navy Flyers Creed

I am a United States Navy flyer.

My countrymen built the best airplane in the world and entrusted it to me. They trained me to fly it. I will use it to the absolute limit of my power. With my fellow pilots, air crews, and deck crews, my plane and I will do anything necessary to carry out our tremendous responsibilities. I will always remember we are part of an unbeatable combat team—the United States Navy.

When the going is fast and rough, I will not falter. I will be uncompromising in every blow I strike. I will be humble in victory.

I am a United States Navy flyer. I have dedicated myself to my country, with its many millions of all races, colors, and creeds. They and their way of life are worthy of my greatest protective effort.

I ask the help of God in making that effort great enough.

Note the penultimate paragraph's reference to dedicating yourself to "all races, colors, and creeds" that make up our great country. My fellow aircrew and I, who represented shades of every skin color, dedicated ourselves to do our best to live up to that creed in 1985. That is one of the reasons why I do not accept or believe that this country is systemically racist.

I thought about asking Martha to marry me after graduating from AOCS. I like to think she would have said yes. In any event, when I did not ask, she did not seem upset. She was not that way, one of the reasons I loved her. She, like I, was brimming with confidence, excitement, and a bit of trepidation about the future. In addition, for my part, I knew that I had only completed the first step of what would be a long, arduous journey. I selfishly wanted to devote all my energy and focus toward successfully completing that journey. Many good men and women graduated from AOCS, Reserve Officer Training Corp (ROTC), or the Naval Academy in Annapolis only to wash out in flight school. I did not plan to be one of them because I was distracted.

I got a letter from Martha while in the middle of the Indian Ocean on my first cruise a little over three years later. She wrote that she was getting married. I was happy for her, but also a bit heartbroken.

CHAPTER 5

FLIGHT SCHOOL

AS OPPOSED TO LEARNING TO fly at Whiting Field in Pensacola as planned, the Navy assigned me to the VT-27 Boomers based at NAS Corpus Christi in Texas for primary flight training. I sold my Sabre 750 and financed a brand-new Toyota Corolla GTS upon graduation from AOCS. Sunroof, leather interior, upgraded stereo, the works. The Navy should have done a better job of educating us about upsells and predatory lending. I drove it, loaded with all my belongings, to Texas' Gulf Coast. My personal belongings at that point consisted of my uniforms and other clothes and my stereo system and albums, complete in 1985 style with two four-foot-tall speakers on which to blast The Beatles, Doors, REM, Black Sabbath, Blondie, and The B-52s.

Dean and I rented a posh apartment in Corpus Christi. We each had our own bedroom and we shared a family room and kitchen. Best yet, the complex had a community pool, gym, and civilians—including girls! It was a short-term, month-to-month lease, as we did not know when we would complete primary and be ordered elsewhere—weather was one of the factors. We rented furniture, sheets, cookware, dishes, etc. Living light is always a good idea, especially when you are living at the whims of the military.

Ground school took up the first month of flight training. We learned about weather, airport operations, communications, and Federal Aviation Administration (FAA) and Navy flight regulations. We also learned all about the T-34 Turbo Mentor, the Navy's fully acrobatic single-engine turboprop trainer at the time. We spent dozens of hours memorizing the location of every instrument on the instrument panel, every switch and circuit breaker, and emergency procedures. We learned how to conduct a thorough preflight check of the aircraft, how to check weather and notices to airmen (NOTAMs), and how to prepare a flight plan and file it with air traffic control. After ground school we were ready to go flying! Lt. Steve Weiss was my primary flight instructor, a nice guy and good teacher.

Flight training began with familiarization flights, learning how to taxi, takeoff, do basic maneuvers, and land safely while communicating with the airport tower and air traffic control. The syllabus included fourteen *fam* flights of between one-and-a-half and two-and-a-half hours each. Every flight had a series of maneuvers you had to perform in the aircraft as you learned to fly. Your instructor graded you on each. I struggled learning how to control the airplane. One thing I could not seem to remember to do after surviving a bumpy takeoff was to raise my landing gear. On my first flight Lt. Weiss gently reminded me.

On my second, he asked, "So, Steve, what do they raise in Michigan?"

"Well, a lot of corn and wheat and some livestock," I responded, while wrestling the aircraft to a safe altitude.

Lt. Weiss replied, in an irritated tone, "In the Navy we raise our landing gear!"

This slow upslope of my learning curve ended up costing me jets, along with a down (a failed training flight) on my seventh fam flight, which required two remedial flights. But I got through and was an adept pilot after those first sixteen flights.

Acrobatics came next. Four flights where you learned to do aileron rolls, barrel rolls, loops, and split S maneuvers. It was a bit intimidating at first to roll the plane upside down. But once inverted, it felt otherworldly to pull the stick back and defy gravity as you cascaded toward the earth in a split S. What a blast!

Following acrobatics, the syllabus required three flights to learn to fly in formation, just a few feet beside and below another airplane. Flying formation was not that hard once tucked in under the lead aircraft. Getting in position was hard and was all about closure. As you approached the lead you got into the proper relative position and then added enough power to close safely while maintaining your alignment. If you were closing too fast you dumped the nose and passed under the lead, dropped back into position, and tried again. Too slow, and the instructor asked, "So, are we going to stay back here forever, or do you plan to get in formation before we run out of fuel?" Our instructors sternly cautioned that if we were to "swap paint" with the other plane, our dreams of flying combat aircraft were over. After formation, we flew two night-familiarization flights.

This all took place in January and February of 1986. Because the weather is stormy on the Texas coast in the spring, we embarked on a detachment to NAS El Centro in California's Imperial Valley to complete primary flight training. We bunked in the Bachelor Officers' Quarters (BOQ) and got to know the area, from the Salton Sea to the north, just south of Coachella, to Calexico and Mexicali to the south. The carne asada tasted terrific.

The Blue Angels did their winter training in El Centro. My fellow students and I watched in awe as they practiced their maneuvers several times a week. In AOCS we learned how Blue Angel pilots would sit in a chair with their eyes closed and visualize the entire flight beforehand, from takeoff to landing, carefully executing every turn, roll, climb, and descent in their head. Watching them perform amazing feats of airmanship in their A-4 Skyhawks reinforced the importance of preparation to us fledgling fliers. Blue Angel pilots, despite being some of the best aviators in the world, have a nearly 10 percent death rate.

From March through May the syllabus called for fourteen flights learning how to fly on instruments. You did this by putting a hood on your helmet that shielded everything but the aircraft instruments. You needed a quick scan and smooth control inputs to fly on instruments well. Most importantly, you needed to be *ahead of the aircraft*, planning for upcoming turns and maneuvers well in advance of when you needed to execute them. Primary culminated in two airway navigation flights, where we learned to safely get from one airport to another and back again without breaking any of the many FAA or Navy regulations.

After primary flight training came the selection process. The Navy assigned all students to one of four main categories of aircraft: jets, helicopters, P-3s, and E-2/C-2s. P-3s are large, fixed-wing aircraft loaded with top-secret electronic equipment. The C-2 Greyhound is the carrier onboard delivery (COD) version of the E-2. C-2s fly people, mail, and supplies out to the carrier. You listed your choices in order of preference. I had recovered from my earlier struggles and was in the top of my class, but not first. If you were first, you got your first choice. Otherwise, the powers that be took your preferences into consideration, along with the needs of the Navy. I listed my choices as 1-jets; 2-helicopters; 3-E-2s; and 4-P-3s. I wanted jets badly, but if I did not get jets, I at least wanted to be on an aircraft carrier—which in the Navy was and still is the *tip of the spear*.

I did not get jets. I got my third choice, E-2s. Grumman Aerospace (which merged with Northrup in 1996) designed the E-2, called the Hawkeye, or Hummer due to the unique sound of its turboprops, in the late 1950s and early 1960s. The E-2 served, and still serves, as the eyes and ears of the fleet, by using radar to detect and identify unknown aircraft (bogies) and ships. It then directs fighters and bombers to intercept them. Its official mission designation is *airborne early warning* (AEW).

A T56-A-427 Allison turboprop engine hung from each wing

of the E-2C. Fifty-seven feet and eight inches long, with an eighty-foot wingspan supporting a twenty-four-foot diameter dome housing a doppler radar, it was and still is the largest aircraft on an aircraft carrier. It takes five crew members to operate: a pilot and copilot up front and three NFOs that sit sideways in the back, each with his own radar screen. There were seven radios in our planes. Gross weight when the wings were full of JP-5 (jet propulsion fuel) was 53,000 pounds. Maximum landing weight on the aircraft carrier was 44,500 pounds. Landing speed was 120 knots. I still remember that, all these years later. I will never forget *Power, Gear, Feather, Flaps, Max Rudder*—the sequence you needed to execute in the event of engine loss, which did not happen often, but did happen.

"Two Airborne Early Warning Squadron 113 (VAW-113) E-2C Hawkeye aircraft fly over the air station during pre-deployment training" National Archives Identifier: 6453500

The E-2's eighty-foot wingspan was necessary to lift its bulk, but not suitable for parking on a crowded aircraft carrier. The carriers then in active service typically housed seventy aircraft.

Today, US aircraft carriers have slightly larger flight decks, but often only house sixty or fewer aircraft due to military spending cutbacks. To account for the lack of space on the decks at the time, the engineers at Grumman designed the wings to break outboard the engines and use hydraulics to fold back and up, attaching to the outward of four vertical stabilizers seated on the tail's horizontal stabilizer. Grumman's initial design only had three vertical stabilizers, each with a movable rudder, but they added a fourth, without a rudder, because the plane looked awkward and asymmetrical with only three.

Another design modification made to fit four E-2s onto a crowded aircraft carrier was its fifty-eight-foot length compared to an eighty-foot wingspan. Grumman designed the plane to be ten feet longer, but a sixty-eight-foot-long aircraft would not fit in an aircraft carrier hangar, so they shortened it. Having designed an aircraft for my senior project at Georgia Tech, I knew that making a plane much shorter than its wingspan exacerbates yaw issues. Yaw is rotation of the aircraft about its vertical axis. Think of a car pulling to the left or right. Roll is rotation about the horizontal axis running from nose to tail. Pitch is rotation about the horizontal axis running wingtip to wingtip.

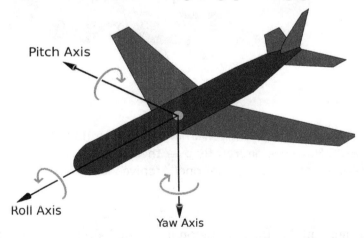

"An image showing all three axises" by Auawise under Creative Commons Attribution-Share Alike 3.0 Unported license

Because the twenty-four-foot diameter radome sits atop the aircraft, over the NFO seats, ejection was not an option. To bail out of the aircraft in flight, you would need to trounce down a narrow passage with a bulky parachute strapped to your back, release the main door into the howling wind, dive out, and pull your ripcord. Fortunately, the E-2 is a reliable aircraft, despite or because of its longevity, and bailouts are exceedingly rare. A crew of four from VAW-121 in Norfolk, Virginia attempted and successfully accomplished the last one in 2020.

The US Navy—as well as Egypt, France, Israel, Japan, Mexico, Singapore, Taiwan, and other allies—still flies the basic airframe of the E-2 today. Back in the early 1990s, the price tag for an E-2C+ was around $90 million. In April of 2019, the Navy awarded Northrup Grumman a $3.2 billion, five-year contract modification to buy twenty-four E-2D Advanced Hawkeyes. That is $133 million each for the latest version of the Hawkeye, which sports significantly upgraded electronics and two curved, eight-bladed propellers instead of the four-blade variable-pitch prop we flew.

I assuaged my ego after not getting jets by seizing on the fact that the unwieldy E-2 was arguably the most difficult aircraft to land on the carrier. Its two props both spun clockwise, which created a significant yaw to the right when you added power. Conversely, when reducing power, the nose pulled to the left. The Navy and Grumman could have eliminated this unfortunate flight characteristic by having the two props spin in opposite directions. But that would have required different props, transmissions, and other parts for the two engines. Space on a carrier is tight. So, they used the same prop on both engines. This reduced the number of spares that the ship needed to carry but, as with the aircraft's shorter length, made the pilot's job more difficult.

You compensated for the yaw induced as you added or pulled power with rudder, which you controlled with pedals. The brakes were at the top of the pedals. If you so much as brushed one of those with the toe of a flight boot upon landing, you blew your tire. Bringing an E-2 aboard a carrier thus involved a firm grip on the yoke (which controlled pitch and roll) with your left hand, operating the throttles with your right hand to keep the plane on glideslope (a steady, 500-foot-per-minute, descending path to touchdown), while your legs worked like mad to keep the nose of the aircraft pointed straight down the centerline of the landing area as you jockeyed the throttles. Herding cats would have undoubtedly been easier.

The E-2s eighty-foot wingspan also meant that when landing on a pitching and rolling aircraft carrier deck at 120 knots, if you touched down just eight feet (10 percent of your wingspan) off the flight deck centerline, your wing would take out the noses of aircraft parked alongside the landing area.

The pipeline to E-2s at the time involved training on two other aircraft, the T-2 Buckeye, a twin-engine jet built by North American Aviation, Inc., and the T-44 Pegasus, a twin-engine turboprop built by Beech Aircraft, now part of Raytheon. The Navy assigned me to the VT-4 Warbucks in Pensacola for T-2 training. Armed with a new set of orders, I loaded up the Corolla and drove back to the Florida Panhandle. I rented a condominium on Perdido Key with fellow ensigns Blaise Duhé, from Louisiana, and John McLaughlin, a Californian. The condo overlooked the sparkling beaches of Perdido Bay, where we swam often.

As with primary, T-2 training started with ground school. The T-2, like the T-34, had a tandem cockpit, with two seats and sets of flight controls, one behind the other. But while the T-34 Turbo Mentor was a single-engine turboprop, the T-2 Buckeye sported two J85-GE-4 turbojet engines, rated at 2,950 pound-feet of thrust each, incorporated into the fuselage. Top speed was 465 knots (535 mph) and you could pull six g's in it. Talk about giving the kids the keys to the candy store.

The T-2 syllabus was intense. You flew nearly every day,

weather permitting, and often had two training flights in a day. The instructors, a mix of navy lieutenants and marine captains, were serious and professional. The syllabus involved twelve familiarization and instrument flights; thirteen formation flights (getting closure right at 250 knots is tricky); a handful of airways navigation and night familiarization hops; and the biggie—carrier qualification. Between August 8 and November 14, 1986, I flew seventy-seven hops in the Buckeye.

In a letter home, I briefly summarized my T-2 training as follows:

UNITED STATES NAVAL AIR STATION
Pensacola, Florida

30 September 1986

All is going well for me here. I'm flying the formation stage now and it is really a lot of fun. We fly four feet below, ten feet beside, and nine feet behind the other aircraft—if this sounds close you should see how close it looks and feels at 250 knots. I had my first solo yesterday and it was really exciting. We are tentatively scheduled to go to the boat Nov. 3 in Key West. This of course is subject to change without notice or reason.

You flew many of the training flights solo, the same with CQ, as we called carrier qualification. Nobody ever explained to me why the Navy did not put an instructor in the back seat to ensure safety, and I never asked. I suspect it was because those of us that successfully CQ'd were likely to become aircraft commanders of combat aircraft in due course. That is a job that requires extreme confidence, both in your ability to fly the aircraft and to make decisions quickly, decisively, and most importantly, correctly. It takes courage to fly out solo to an aircraft carrier and attempt your first landing on a boat. Anything can happen.

Thunderstorms often formed over Pensacola in the afternoon. Cumulonimbus clouds would start to build up around 1600, followed by lightning and pelting rain for an hour or two, suspending flight operations. As naval aviators, our instructors trained us to fly in all weather. But they also trained us not to take stupid risks with our life or aircraft. Flying in a thunderstorm when you do not have to is a stupid risk. But those towering clouds were fun to play with before they turned dark, damp, and charged with lightning. On solos I would wrap the jet around a cloud trying to gently brush its gossamer edges with the top of my canopy as I pulled back hard on the stick. I used every bit of that plane's capability, all six g's and 465 knots.

The maintenance officer reprimanded me once, after I got carried away and exceeded the plane's six-g limit. The plane's g-meter tracked the maximum g-force you pulled on a flight. Maintenance checked it postflight. Overstressing the aircraft required extra tests and documentation. My exuberance created additional work for the maintenance team, and I never repeated the error.

I did lose control of a T-2 one afternoon while practicing acrobatics. Leveling out after a few barrels roll and still doing 300 knots, I pulled up into a loop. I was sloppy on the way up and bled too much airspeed. The plane ran out at the top. Inverted, we stalled and went into a spin. As I slammed against the sides of the cockpit, watching my altimeter spin downward, I realized, *This is not good.*

Falling back on my training, I neutralized the spin by holding the stick steady and applying rudder opposite its direction. Still inverted, rather than push the stick forward (as we had read about but never practiced) I pulled back to break the stall. It worked.

After recovering control, I realized I had dropped over 2,000 feet below the prescribed 10,000-foot hard deck. Fortunately, the T-2 did not have a spin-meter and nobody asked. I was not inclined to tell.

For the most part, we students did not think about dying in an airplane crash. While we recognized the possibility, it seemed remote, especially given our extensive training. Most of my fellow flight students came from middle- to lower-middle- class backgrounds, and we did not feel that the world owed us anything. But the United States of America provided opportunities we would not enjoy elsewhere and we eagerly seized upon them.

Being sent out to fly a jet daily, often alone, to hone your skills built great confidence. Midway through T-2 training, while I respected the aircraft greatly, my fears largely dissipated. After securing a g-suit—which would inflate around my torso, thighs, and calves while pulling sustained g's and coupled with a Kegel squeeze helped to prevent blackout—over my fire-resistant flight suit, cinching into a flight harness, squeezing into the narrow cockpit, connecting my g-suit and oxygen mask, buckling into the ejection seat, pulling the safety pin, and grasping the throttles with my left hand and the stick between my legs with my right, feet firmly on the rudder pedals—the aircraft became an extension of my body, subject to my will. At that point, we began preparing to test our growing confidence at the carrier.

Preparing for carrier qualification involved ten training flights and a minimum of seventy-five FCLPs (field carrier landing practice). The landing area on an aircraft carrier was a little under one hundred feet wide and around 720 feet long—about a third narrower and twice the length of a football field. Four 1 3/8-inch diameter, six-stranded arresting cables, each with a minimum breaking strength of 188,000 pounds, stretched across the landing area at forty-foot intervals. Massive Mark 7 arresting engines below deck allowed the cables to play out gently enough to not rip the tailhook off the aircraft, yet strongly enough to bring a twenty-ton plane to a stop in a little under 400 feet. The distance between the one wire and the four wire (as we called the arresting cables) was 120 feet.

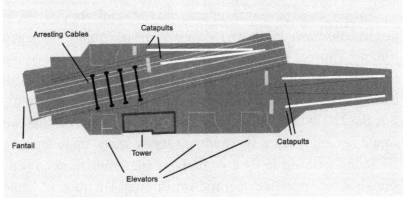

Aerial view of the flight deck of the USS *Constellation*, CV-64. Drawing courtesy of Braden Waller, Big Squid Studios.

Glideslope was critical when trying to plant your landing gear on an undulating 120-foot stretch of steel while traveling at 120 (E-2) or 150 knots (fighters and bombers). Unlike when you fly into your local airport and the pilot greases the wheels down on the ten-thousand-foot runway after a smooth, long flare and taxies to your gate, when landing on a carrier you flew a five-hundred-foot-per-minute rate of descent all the way into the teeth-rattling collision with the flight deck. Then, hopefully, you slammed forward into your harness straps to the point of bruising as the cable brought the aircraft to a stop on the remaining strip of steel.

If you did not feel the eight or so g's (nearly instantaneous) as the plane's tailhook grabbed a cable, you had *boltered*. A bolter occurred after you saw the approaching flight deck, including the fantail that dropped from the rear of the ship and loomed large and dangerous in your windscreen. You added a little power to make sure you did not crash into the fantail or have it rip off your landing gear or tailhook. That little bit of extra power caused you to touch down beyond the four wire (the sweet spot was the forty feet from just before the two wire to the three wire) and quickly depart the flight deck you were planning to park upon. This was obviously not a desired or successful outcome. But it was preferable to crashing into the fantail.

A bolter was always a possibility, sometimes even when you flew a flawless approach but the pitching carrier deck did not cooperate. As a result, upon feeling the jolt of a five-hundred-foot-per-minute impact, you added full power to the aircraft engines just in case you needed to get airborne again. This practice, and the terror of your first few *traps*, as aviators call carrier arrested landings, sometimes led pilots to forget to power down after a successful landing. This resulted in more than one air boss radioing down from the carrier's tower:

"Hey! Aircraft in the landing area. You can throttle down. You're not making the ship go any faster."

To facilitate flying a steady glideslope down to the carrier, pilots used a MK 6 Mod 3 Fresnel lens affixed to the port side of the landing area. A horizontal row of blue lights, or datum, bisected the five vertical cells in the center of the lens. The top four vertical cells were yellow. The bottom cell was red. Only one lens was lit at a time. We called the illuminated lens *the meatball*, or simply *the ball*. When on glideslope, the middle lens was lit and in line with the datum lights. If you drifted high, the meatball would drift up to the next cell and the next until you were so high it disappeared off the top. Likewise, if you were low, the meatball shifted down to the yellow and then the red cell below the datum. If you went below the red cell, you were probably going to crash.

The MK 6 MOD 3 Fresnel Lens Optical Landing System on the port side of the ship provides pilots with critical glideslope information. Public domain image by DoDMedia.

In the picture the airplane is one ball low. At three quarters of a mile, when you *called the ball*, each cell's vertical beam height was twenty-seven feet. When crossing the fantail, it was three feet. Two vertical rows of red lights on either side of the vertical center cells were the wave off lights. A landing signal officer (LSO) stood on a platform on the port side of the ship, toward the stern. The LSO held a radio in one hand (picture an old-fashioned telephone receiver with a transmit button) and a trigger to control the wave off lights in the other. LSOs used the radio to *wave* planes aboard with simple commands: "You're high," "You're low," "Power," "Come left," "Right for lineup," and of course "Wave off."

The term *waving* the planes aboard comes from the days of the first, wooden-decked aircraft carriers. LSOs held a large paddle in each hand and waved them to provide signals to help guide the pilots aboard. Aviators refer to LSOs as *paddles* to this day. An angled net hung over the ocean beside the LSO platform. LSOs could dive into the net and roll beneath the steel flight deck in the event a plane crashed into the fantail. In my mind, the odds of getting to the net before the fireball and shattered steel travelled the 300 feet to the LSO platform seemed only slightly better than those of surviving a nuclear attack by hiding under your desk.

I became an LSO upon entering the fleet and waved plenty of dangerous landings. The scariest involved an F-14 Tomcat on my first cruise. F-14 engines were notorious for taking a second or two to spool back up after the pilot pulled too much power. You could hear it before seeing it, which is why I did not wear an ear plug in my left ear while on the LSO platform and my high frequency hearing in that ear is shot.

That night, the pitch of the Tomcat's engines increased and the fighter jet rose above glideslope before, eerily, its engines' roar became a whisper. Upon hearing this, instead of telling the pilot he was high, as I was about to, I pressed the transmit button on the headset held against my left ear and commanded, "Power! Wave off!" while simultaneously squeezing the trigger in my right hand to initiate the wave off lights. The pilot responded by slamming the throttles forward, but it was too late. The plane sank and the pilot saw the ball fall through the bottom, red cell of the lens. His landing gear cleared the fantail by inches, but his tailhook did not. Miraculously, instead of ripping off, the tailhook bounced off the fantail and grabbed the one-wire when it came back down. Even then, none of us on the LSO platform dove into the safety net. We only did that for fun, after getting all the planes safely aboard.

The final parameter you had to fly properly, along with glideslope and centerline, was angle of attack (the pitch of the aircraft). E-2s landed at a twenty-degree angle of attack, nose twenty degrees above the horizontal plane. An angle-of-attack indicator, affixed to the top of the instrument panel (on the left, just to the right of where you viewed the ball through the windscreen) consisted of a yellow circle with chevrons above and below. As with the Fresnel lens, an illuminated yellow ball in the middle was the sweet spot. If your angle of attack was high, the upper chevron was lit. If it was low, the lower chevron illuminated. If your angle of attack got too high, a stall-warning buzzer signaled that you were about to lose the lift that kept your aircraft aloft.

LSOs graded every FCLP and every carrier landing. Squadrons posted all carrier landing grades prominently in the ready room, where the aircrew assembled for briefings, for all to see. LSOs awarded an *OK* for a good, smooth, safe pass—worth four points. A *fair* pass was smooth and safe, but with a small deviation or two from glideslope or centerline, and worth three points. Next was the dreaded *bolter*, when the pilot overshot all the wires and bounced back into the sky to reenter the landing pattern—two-and-a-half points. A pass that was safe, but ugly, earned a *no grade*—two points. LSOs ordered a *wave off* if they decided the plane was coming in with unsettled dynamics in a potentially unsafe manner and hit the lights, telling the pilot to add full power, go around the landing pattern, and try again, harder—one point. Last and least was the zero-point *cut pass*, awarded when a plane made unsafe deviations within the wave-off window.

I gave the Tomcat pilot that *hook-slapped* on my first cruise a cut pass. Charlie was a friend and none too happy about it. (Although he bought me a beer and thanked me as we clinked glasses a couple of weeks later in Australia.) There was also the exceedingly rare five-point underlined *OK*, for bringing an aircraft safely aboard with serious complicating factors, such as an engine out. If a pilot flew a cut pass, or more than a handful of bolters, wave offs, or no grade landings in his one hundred plus traps on a cruise, caught too many one wires, or if his grade point average fell below a 3.0, he was likely to find himself trying to explain to his squadron commanding officer (skipper) and the carrier air group commander (CAG) why he should not be selling insurance.

I carrier qualified on November 2 and 3 of 1986, aboard the USS *Lexington*, CV-16, commissioned in 1943. Two fellow student aviators and I flew our jets out to the carrier in a four-plane formation on the wing of an instructor. We flew into the *break* to enter the landing pattern, an imaginary horizontal oval at 600 feet altitude with the carrier in the center right. As the lead aircraft passed the bow of the carrier at 300 knots it sharply banked left sixty degrees and decelerated through a 180-degree turn while maintaining altitude—the *break*. The other three aircraft in the formation followed suit at twenty-second intervals, setting up a one-minute separation between planes.

Rolling out of my turn into the downwind leg of the approach (the carrier steams into the wind during flight operations) I lowered my landing gear and flaps and slowed to landing speed. When *abeam* the landing area, you needed to be all set up to fly a descending, twenty- to twenty-five-degree angle-of-bank left turn to final approach. The speed of the carrier steaming into the wind created a three-quarter mile separation from the ship during your approach turn. Rolling out on final, hopefully on glideslope and centerline, you called the ball.

I set myself up the correct distance abeam the carrier, right at 600 feet altitude, gear and flaps down, and at the proper angle-of-attack and airspeed. Pulling power, I started the 180-degree, descending turn into final approach. Completing my turn to final I pressed the transmit button and called "Buckeye ball." It was a ball high. I pulled power to bring the aircraft down to glideslope. As the ball settled into the middle cell, I worked furiously, making small throttle and stick adjustments to maintain centerline and angle of attack.

As the jet closed on the flight deck, the ball started to climb, rapidly. I again pulled power, a little too aggressively. My T-2 and I slammed into the flight deck at around six- to seven-hundred-feet-per-minute, its tailhook grabbing the four wire. And I am eternally grateful that it did.

My hard landing caused the metal bracket holding the right side of the instrument panel to the plane's fuselage to shear. The heavy panel landed in my lap, pinning the stick all the way back into my crotch and abdomen. If I had boltered on that pass, my plane would have gone straight up, stalled, and crashed. Worse, it probably would have done so right back onto the flight deck, killing not just me but some of the hundred or so sailors working there.

As I throttled back and the arresting cable brought the jet to a stop, I glanced skyward and gave a quick thanks to God. A yellow shirt (aircraft handler) signaled to raise my tailhook by moving one thumb up into an open palm. Flight deck personnel wear colored shirts, designating their role. Green shirts maintain the catapults and arresting cables, as well as the engines that power them. Purple shirts fuel the aircraft. Blue shirts operate the elevators and chock and chain planes. Red shirts handle armaments. Safety personnel wear white shirts. Plane captains, who are responsible for the aircraft when it is not flying, wear brown shirts. Most pilots acknowledge that the twenty-one-year-old plane captain owns the aircraft—you just borrow it.

As I lifted the lever to raise the hook, it dropped the wire and the yellow shirt started directing me to taxi out of the landing area. I screwed up my courage, pressed the radio transmit button, and called the air boss. The air boss was a Navy commander who had already served as a squadron CO and was responsible for all aspects of operations involving aircraft on the hangar deck, flight deck, and within five nautical miles of the carrier.

"Uh, boss," I stammered. "I've got a problem. My instrument panel is in my lap."

After a short silence, the boss responded with a crisp, "All right, get the hell out of my landing area and we'll deal with it."

I taxied clear and parked in the shadow of Primary Flight Ops (the tower where the air boss worked) while two blue shirts threw chocks around my wheels with the engines running.

The plan had been to taxi to the catapult and launch for additional traps. Instead, I raised my canopy and a different yellow shirt rolled a ladder up to the cockpit, climbed up, looked at the detached instrument panel, and left without saying a word. Speaking would have been pointless anyway because the deafening sound of jet engines at full power as flight operations continued would have required me to know how to read lips.

I had no idea what was going on but was not eager to radio the air boss again during the middle of CQ to ask. A few minutes later, the yellow shirt returned to the cockpit with a roll of bailing wire, a lopsided grin, and a thumbs up. *No way!* I thought, *he's planning to wire the instrument panel back to the fuselage and send me to the catapult.* That sounded like suicide—counting on bailing wire to survive a catapult shot—and I said so by shaking my head, vehemently. Calmer heads prevailed and the boss ordered me to shut down.

After an hour or so, one of my fellow students finished for the day. I *hot seated* into his jet (switched pilots with engines running) to get some work in towards the goal of ten traps and three touch-and-gos (landing with the tail hook up).

My first catapult shot was a rush. So was taxiing to the catapult. The chaos of a flight deck simultaneously launching and recovering aircraft is controlled through strict procedures. An aircraft never moves on the flight deck unless under a yellow shirt's control. Yellow shirts never move when directing aircraft. This prevents the illusion that an aircraft is moving when it's not (especially crucial at night). When an aircraft reaches the yellow shirt controlling it, he passes it to the next handler by pointing to him. Pilots must taxi at idle power or their exhaust may knock flight deck personnel down or even off the deck. Yellow shirts pass signals to pilots above the waist. They give signals to others on the flight deck below the waist to limit confusion.

I approached the No. 1 catapult on the starboard side of the bow under the direction of a final yellow shirt. The launch director put an elbow in his palm (it looks like he is giving you the bird) and lowered his forearm, signaling me to lower the launch bar. After carefully taxiing into the catapult shuttle, a blue shirt raised a steel exhaust deflector behind me and another attached a holdback fitting to my launch bar. Once in the catapult, I added power (the only time it is allowed on a flight deck) and taxied forward the last two feet. After looking fore and aft to clear the area, the yellow shirt raised his right palm, telling me to release the brakes. He then pointed his left arm straight forward, indicating to take tension. As the plane's nose squatted into position, I realized I was now a bullet in a gun that was about to be fired.

Once in tension, the yellow-shirted *shooter,* an officer responsible for the catapult, gave the *run-up* signal by waving an outstretched arm in the air vigorously. Advancing the throttles all the way forward, I grasped the T-shaped bar that prevents you from pulling back on the throttles due to the force of the catapult shot. I *wiped* the controls by cycling the stick and rudder pedals to their limits and noting the appropriate movements of the ailerons, elevators, and rudder. A final scan of the instruments looked good, so I gave a salute to the shooter and quickly regrasped the stick with my right hand while maintaining full power with my left.

The catapult fired and eight g's of force pressed me back into the seat as the plane accelerated to flying speed in 300 feet. Darkness overtook my peripheral vision as I squeezed my abdomen and grunted against the g's. Upon clearing the flight deck, my vision returned instantly and I executed a quick right turn so that if I had to eject or ditch, the 88,000-ton carrier would not run me over.

After two touch-and-gos and a second, uneventful, trap, I

taxied back to the catapult, launched, and flew the jet back to Pensacola. With the sun setting over the Gulf of Mexico behind me, I reflected on a remarkable day and thought about how to fly smoother passes tomorrow.

I completed CQ in two flights that second day, five traps and a touch-and-go on the first and three traps on the second. No bolters. With that I joined some of the finest aviators in the world as a United States Navy carrier pilot.

The LSO gave me a no grade on my first carrier landing when the instrument panel bracket sheared. A fair grade, in that the pass was ugly and the plane broke. But the T-2s were toward the end of their service life and I would bet that there were hairline stress fractures or worse in that bracket from the thousands of prior carrier landings it had endured. In any event, I am grateful that the Navy did not wash me out at that point. The Navy sent a handful of pilots who did not make it through CQ home or into a different specialty.

Carrier qualification complete, I finished the T-2 syllabus in a couple of more flights and then shipped back to Training Wing Four in Corpus Christi to fly the T-44 Pegasus. T-44 training taught E-2 pilots how to fly a twin-engine turboprop with one engine out. Jet pilots learned single engine procedures as well, but because engineers typically placed jet engines close to the aircraft's centerline, flight dynamics did not change as much as they did when your engines hung several feet out on the wing and one of them suddenly stopped providing thrust. I lived in the BOQ and completed ground school and the eleven-flight syllabus between late November 1986 and mid-January 1987.

The T-44 had a side-by-side cockpit and two passenger seats, allowing one instructor to take up two students and have them take turns performing the maneuvers required by the syllabus. It was fun to watch friend and fellow student Jeff Kilmer, a former place kicker for Ole Miss, go through his maneuvers—less fun having him critically watch me do my best to perform mine. We both wanted to go last so that we could use the other's turn as a primer. I enjoyed flying the T-44, but I missed the speed and power of the T-2. After flying the E-2, Jeff detached to the Marines and flew the AV-8B Harrier, the first VTOL (vertical takeoff and landing) fighter/attack jet of its kind, before flying for FedEx.

The Navy awarded us our gold wings upon completion of flight school. A *jody* often sung by students in AOCS while double-timing around the base went as follows:

I don't know but I've been told. Navy wings are made of gold.

I don't know but it's been said. Air Force wings are made of lead.

My dad flew out to Corpus Christi for the winging ceremony, which took place in the officers' club. Our instructors did not present us with the coveted wings of gold on a satin pillow with lace trim or anything so civilized. Instead, per Navy tradition, an instructor dropped your hard-earned, golden wings (Air Force wings are pewter colored) into a pitcher of beer, which you had to drink to retrieve them. To do this properly, you chugged the pitcher and caught the wings in your teeth at the end. My experience on the Delta Tau Delta beer drinking team, which, anchored by Doug Davis, won the competition held in the Agora Ballroom in Atlanta, came in handy. Afterwards, one of your instructors or classmates pinned the wings to your chest by placing the two brass prongs on the back of the wings on your left breast and hammering them in with a sharp smack of the palm.

Having earned my wings and become a naval aviator, the time arrived for assignment to the RAG (Replacement Air Group—a fleet aircraft training squadron, also called a fleet replacement squadron). This time my desires and the needs of the Navy aligned. The Department of the Navy assigned me to the West Coast E-2C RAG, Carrier Airborne Early Warning Squadron VAW-110. The letters in a squadron's official name indicate distinct aspects of its type and purpose. The V, in VAW-110 and VT-27, denotes fixed wing aircraft. Helicopter squadron designations begin with an H. The remaining letters identify the mission. Hawkeye squadrons were thus designated VAW, for fixed wing, airborne early warning. T stands for training. F is for fighter, A is for attack (bombers), AQ stands for attack, electronic, and S is for submarine hunters.

The VAW-110 Firebirds shared NAS Miramar, located north of San Diego and nicknamed *Fightertown USA*, with the West Coast's E-2 and F-14 fleet squadrons, as well as the Navy's Fighter Weapons School, highlighted in the 1986 movie *Top Gun*. The East Coast RAG is at NAS Norfolk, in Virginia. Fun fact—the producers of *Top Gun* chose the VAW-110 squadron patch, featuring a red Firebird swooping down with its talons extended on a blue background, as the patch worn by Tom Cruise's fictional VF-1 squadron in the film.

CHAPTER 6

FLEET REPLACEMENT SQUADRON
TRAINING

IN JANUARY OF 1987, MY trusty Corolla carried me and all my belongings from Texas to California, where I reported to VAW-110. I had lived in a barracks in Pensacola from July through October 1985, Corpus Christi from November to May 1986 (with a three-month detachment to El Centro, CA in the middle), Pensacola again from June to November 1986, back to Corpus Christi for the rest of November and December, and then moved myself and all my belongs to California. Seven moves in a year and a half.

Flight training did not get any easier in the RAG. The E-2 is a large, sophisticated aircraft. United States Navy fleet aircraft are some of the best designed and engineered aircraft in the world. I looked forward to tackling the task of learning how to operate one.

Blaise, Paul Nevins, and I rented a small house on Winchat Street in Linda Vista, CA. Paul hailed from California and had long (for the Navy) blond hair, so we called him "Gnarly." The house was just a mile from the University of San Diego, where I would later attend law school after leaving the Navy. More importantly, it was only a few miles east of Mission Beach and the Beachcomber, our favorite Sunday afternoon haunt. Gnarly bought himself a Kawasaki crotch rocket and I had motorcycle envy. In addition to Blaise and Gnarly, my Firebird classmates included Dave Busse, Andy Dressel, Adam Ferreira, Darryl Long, and Curtis Phillips.

The NATOPS (Naval Air Training and Operations Standardization) manual was a naval aviator's operational bible. The E-2C manual was 700 pages long. It had eleven sections: The Aircraft; Indoctrination; Normal Procedures; Flight Characteristics; Emergency Procedures; All Weather Operations; Communications Procedures; Weapons Systems; Flight Crew Coordination; NATOPS Evaluation; and Performance Characteristics. It also included various charts and tables in the back. You needed to read and understand everything in the manual and memorize emergency procedures and various other information. As with the training aircraft, you had to be able to locate every instrument on the panel and every individual circuit breaker (there were around one hundred in the E-2) blindfolded. My fellow students and I may have been dumb, wannabe jet jockeys, but we knew our aircraft and its systems.

RAG instructors earned their positions by excelling in the fleet. Consummate professionals, the Navy tasked them with teaching us the art of safely and effectively operating a $90 million aircraft with a crew of five and an important mission. They each took pride in teaching us well. Baron Asher, Roger Chapa, Dave Louzek, and other exemplary instructors helped get us through the demanding RAG syllabus.

Prior to flying the E-2, we attended SERE (Survival, Evasion, Resistance, and Escape) school for two weeks in April of 1987. The Navy's SERE School was in Warner Springs, California, in the Cleveland National Forest. Three of the final five days of SERE training we spent in the field. After a day practicing survival techniques and navigation, we set out to try to make our way to the rally point while avoiding capture. Everyone failed and spent the final day and a half in a mock prisoner of war (POW) camp.

Our instructors told us not to discuss SERE school with

civilians. But national security will not be impacted if I relay that my friend Dave Busse ("Busman") escaped the POW camp on the final day, stole an ambulance that was standing by for emergencies, and drove it back into the camp through the front gates. That stunt earned him the peanut butter and jelly sandwich and ice-cold Coca-Cola promised to any successful escapee. It also earned him the chance to come back and do SERE school again, without embarrassing his instructors this time. Busman tells me that he does not regret his adventure outside the POW camp gates. Nor should he. He is a legend. I also completed Jungle Survival Training in December of 1988, and the week-long Advanced SERE course in October of 1989.

We did not get to fly the E-2 until mid-May. Because the E-2 was a different animal than the trainers we had flown previously, we took it slowly at first. I flew two training flights in May, seven in June, and six in July, as I learned how to handle the aircraft. The size of the plane and the fact that you sat side by side with a copilot, a couple of feet left of the aircraft centerline (in the smaller T-44 it was only several inches), made learning to taxi more difficult than I expected. We ramped up to sixteen flights in August. I did my cross-country qualification at the end of the month, flying from Miramar to Norfolk, Virginia and back with instructor Ray Crouse, another student, and a young petty officer.

In September we started FCLPs in the E-2. We would fly four or five planes to El Centro or out to San Clemente Island, eighty miles off the coast. Once there, we took turns practicing carrier landings while an instructor in the right seat provided coaching and an LSO on the runway graded each pass. I logged 132 FCLPs before flying out to the carrier and bagging five touch-and-gos (three at night) and seventeen traps (seven at night) October 6–8, 1987. Embarrassingly, my Aviators Flight Logbook also shows that I had three bolters (one at night). Wrestling an E-2 onto the deck of an aircraft carrier, even in calm seas and clear skies, is akin to wrestling a bear.

As reflected in my final fitness report from VAW-110, written in all caps on an IBM *Selectric* typewriter and signed by the CO, Commander Mitch Highfill:

> ENS MCKENNA WAS ASSIGNED TO THIS COMMAND FOR DUTY UNDER INSTRUCTION UNDERGOING TRANSITIONAL TRAINING TO THE HIGHLY COMPLEX E-2 AIRCRAFT. HIS TRAINING CONSISTED OF 412 HOURS OF ACADEMIC TRAINING, 50 HOURS OF FLIGHT SIMULATORS AND 64 HOURS OF FLIGHT TRAINING. HE DILIGENTLY PREPARED FOR EACH EVOLUTION AND WAS HIGHLY RECEPTIVE TO INSTRUCTION. ENS MCKENNA SUCCESSFULLY COMPLETED THE ASSIGNED COURSE OF INSTRUCTION IN AN EXCELLENT MANNER.

Now came the time to put the previous twenty-seven-months of training to work.

AOCS Regimental Commander, October 1985

A satisfying first salute from Gy.Sgt. Crenshaw, USMC, NCOIC,
a great teacher

Newly commissioned Ensign McKenna, 1985

Bracing for a shot off the starboard catapult

Cockpit view of the fantail on final approach

USS Constellation CV-64

Our bedroom aboard ship was the size of a high ceilinged coffin

CV-64 enlisted berthing space

I will never forget manning the rails as we sailed past the sunken battleship USS *Arizona* and into Pearl Harbor on December 13, 1988

FOD walkdown? Why the helmets?

The VAW-113 Black Eagle officers on the *Connie*'s flight deck

Flying amidst the mountains in the Aelutian Island Chain,
May 1989

The wind sock at Shemya Air Force Base, Alaska, where we were stranded for three days

Showing Dad the hangar deck on Tiger Cruise, May 27 to June 1, 1989

Friends and fellow aviators make a sword arch to welcome
Patricia to the Navy

Patricia and I cut the wedding cake with my sword from AOCS

Me and my groomsmen. Back row: Kurt, Scott, Paul, Brian Charles, Charlie. Front: Otis and Spike

It was extremely cool when I got my name on a plane

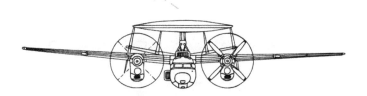

SECTION III:
SERVING IN THE FLEET

CHAPTER 7

BRIEFLY A SEA BAT BEFORE JOINING
THE BLACK EAGLES

AFTER GRADUATING FROM THE RAG, the Navy issued me orders to the VAW-111 Seabats, led by Commander Chuck Breitigam, a great pilot and leader whom I remember well. He had gray hair (as I do now) and a full, bushy mustache (something I have tried and failed to grow many times).

My last flight in VAW-110 was on October 14 and my first in VAW-111 was less than a week later, on October 20. Dave Louzek, one of my many great RAG instructors, was now a lieutenant commander and Seabat department head. The executive officer (XO) was Commander Pfeiffer, also a fantastic pilot and teacher. Lieutenant Juan Grado, the squadron LSO, took me under his wing and brought me into the fraternity of landing signal officers. He got me orders to do two weeks of LSO training school in Norfolk, Virginia that December. The patch from the school that the VAW-111 parachute riggers stitched to my leather flight jacket carries the school's motto: *Rectum Non Bustus*—an apt motto given the LSO's role. Some of my classmates and I employed it while *urban surfing* around base on the roof of our white loaner panel van *ala* Michael J. Fox in *Teen Wolf* one night. As with all the Navy schools and trainings I attended, the work was demanding. But I got to befriend a talented group of pilots from across the air wing as we learned the technicalities of our unique side profession.

I flew a lot with Dave, Juan, XO Pfeiffer, and Skipper Breitigam over the next few months, as they took my RAG training to the next level. We got the unwelcome news that the Department of the Navy had decided to stand down (disband) VAW-111 in early 1988. The Navy originally disestablished VAW-111 in 1976, following Vietnam. It then reestablished it in October of 1986, toward the end of President Reagan's Cold War military build-up, only to change its mind less than a year and a half later.

My last flight as a Seabat was with Juan, on February 1. I went skiing the following week at Squaw Valley (now known as Palisades Tahoe), took a bad fall, and fractured my left fibula. Unable to put any weight on that leg, I skied down on the other, relying heavily on my ski poles. When I got back to Miramar to see the flight surgeon, he put me in a cast and on no-fly status for six weeks. It took a while to get the hang of operating the clutch of my manual transmission with a crutch. At the end of February, the Navy reassigned all the Seabats. I received orders to report to the VAW-113 Black Eagles, with whom I would deploy on two Western Pacific cruises (WestPacs).

The Black Eagles were a great bunch. I reunited with Darryl, Curtis, Andy, and Adam from the RAG and quickly became friends with all the other junior officers (JOs). However, in something that has rarely happened in my career, Navy or otherwise, the skipper, Commander Rocco Ersek, and I did not get along. I remember standing in his office receiving my first fitness report (how the Navy evaluates its officers and enlisted) as a Black Eagle and being told:

"If you were standing in a room and shit was falling down from the ceiling on your head, you would just stand there," insinuating that I did not step up into leadership positions when I should.

Perhaps he was right, as I just stood there. I did not agree with Skipper Ersek but was too shocked to tell him so. The fitness report itself was not bad, it just was not exceptionally good. He gave me a B in forcefulness and did not recommend me for early promotion. I did not complain to anyone or demand that my grade be changed to what I thought I deserved, but I did vow to show the skipper that I could shovel shit—his or anybody else's—with the best of them.

Cdr. Ersek rotated out of the Black Eagles shortly after that and the Navy promoted Commander Christopher J. Remshak from executive to commanding officer. Cdr. Remshak was a mentor whom I respected greatly. He ran a tight ship, demanding your best efforts and solid results. But he also knew how to have fun and realized that the stress of our jobs made letting off steam on occasion a necessary relief valve.

Cdr. Remshak and Cdr. Ersek were NFOs. The squadron pilots designated as carrier aircraft plane commanders (CAPCs) flew with the newbies like me. Commander Brad Gregor, the XO, Lieutenant Commanders Don Tomasoski ("Ski") and Rich Payne, along with Lieutenants Rich Elder and Bob Reifsnyder ("Reif"), continued my education as an E-2 pilot.

I put 10 percent down on a VA loan and bought my first house in May of 1988, on Lolin Lane in Poway, California for $117,500. That was a huge amount on my paltry salary as a Navy lieutenant junior grade—around $2,000 a month in basic pay, plus flight pay and allowances for quarters and sustenance—but I figured California real estate was a sound investment and I could swing it. It was a two-bedroom, 1,600 square foot bungalow with a kidney shaped pool in the small back yard. My parents came out to visit and helped me tear out a chicken wire enclosure in back that had obviously been an aviary given the mess. We installed a garage door opener, put in a sprinkler system, and did some painting to spruce the place up. I ill-advisedly glued AstroTurf to the small concrete patio in the back yard.

That December we were due to embark on a six-month Western Pacific cruise as part of Carrier Air Wing (CVW) 14 aboard the USS *Constellation,* CV-64. I decided I would rent out the house while deployed and hired a property management company. For a mere 10 percent of the rent, they found a tenant and managed the property in my absence. The 90 percent I received barely covered the mortgage, let alone the new hot water heater and furnace the property manager installed in the six-months I was gone.

It could take two weeks to get mail out to the carrier, and two weeks for a letter to get back, so I had given the property manager power of attorney over the house. Not only did I not make any money after having to buy the water heater and furnace, when I got back from cruise the next June, I discovered that the tenants had multiple cats and apparently no litter box. I had to replace the urine-soaked carpeting. The tenants had bailed out, knowing their $1,000 security deposit would not come close to covering the damage.

CHAPTER 8

WESTPAC DECEMBER 1988–JUNE 1989:
AN INAUSPICIOUS START

GOING ON A SIX-MONTH CRUISE took a lot of preparation, both personally and professionally. Personally, you needed to make sure bills got paid, someone cared for your property, etc. If you had a spouse, she or he had to take care of things while you were halfway around the world working on a ship. It was hazardous duty, especially on an aircraft carrier—one of the most dangerous work environments on the planet, even in the absence of armed conflict. I was seeing a nice gal at the time I began preparing for my first cruise but broke off the relationship before deploying. Neither one of us needed the stress.

We called the period prior to cruise *work ups*. Pilots completed FCLPs, followed by carrier qualification. You got a small taste of living on a ship during work ups, especially as an LSO. Every pilot in the entire CVW-14 Air Wing needed to CQ: two F-14A (Tomcat) fighter squadrons; two F/A-18 (Hornet) fighter/attack squadrons; an A-6E (Intruder) bomber squadron; an EA-6B (Prowler) electronic warfare squadron; an S-3A (Viking) sub hunter squadron; and an E-2C (Hawkeye) squadron, as well as an SH-3H (Sea King) helicopter squadron. That was a lot of pilots to get qualified before deploying. To accomplish that task, LSOs stayed on the boat overnight for a couple of nights every other week or so in the month or two before deployment.

Recovering aircraft while on cruise usually involved twelve to fifteen aircraft, twenty at most. Even with a bolter or two thrown in, you were usually on and off the LSO platform in under half an hour. During CQ, the carrier spent hours continuously launching and recovering aircraft to get over a hundred air wing pilots the ten traps (four at night) each needed. Upon hitting my rack around two in the morning—after a second four-hour stint on the flight deck, a deliciously greasy mess deck slider, and some soft-serve ice cream with chocolate sauce—the residual adrenaline would lose its fight against exhaustion and the waves would rock me into a deep sleep filled with amazingly vivid, sometimes disturbing, dreams.

As our December 1, 1988, departure date approached, the *black shoes* (ship's company wore black shoes as part of their uniform) got the carrier and other ships supplied with weapons, fuel, food, and other supplies. The air wing personnel (*brown shoes*) got carrier qualified and started to move their personal belongings aboard to the staterooms they would call home for the next six months. I ended up living in a six-man stateroom—picture a two-person college dorm with three sets of bunk beds, and six small desks and lockers.

Aviators give each other call signs. These can be based on their name, (such as the one given to CVW-14 LSO Jeff Bates, callsign "Master"), your resemblance to a famous person or character, a funny story, or anything else. My JO roommates were Darryl Long ("Spike," a fullback at Santa Clara and an invitee to the San Francisco 49ers mini-camp, was built like one), Adam Ferreira ("Junior," although at the time Adam's call sign was "Psycho," after the character in the movie *Stripes*. We did not settle on "Junior"—Jackie Gleeson's jilted son in *Smokey and the Bandit*—until mid-cruise), Andy Dressel ("Sausage," use your imagination, a good golfer from California who once painted aptly named Doobie Brother Michael McDonald's house, while

Mr. McDonald worked in his garage, where he kept his bong and his Grammy Awards), Wes Spidell ("Spud," a large, jovial, potato shaped genius whom I made the mistake of wrestling, once), and Curtis Phillips, who was from Oklahoma and "farm to table" white, so we named him after the lead singer of Otis Day and the Knights from the movie *Animal House*—"Otis, my man!"

Spike dubbed me "Clyde," after the trouble-causing orangutan featured in the Clint Eastwood *Every Which Way But Loose* movies. We called our compact living quarters the *six-pack*. A disparate, dedicated group, you could not pick better guys to live with in such close quarters for six months. As JOs, we would all work toward our CAPC (pilot) and Mission Commander (NFO) qualifications over the next couple of months.

The six-pack was cramped, but preferable to the enlisted quarters that housed scores of sailors on slender bunkbeds. Most of the enlisted men on the carrier worked twelve-hour shifts. Thus, one bunk could accommodate two sailors on alternate shifts. They called the practice *hot racking*. At least when I crawled into my rack and under the sheet after a long day in the cockpit or on the flight deck, I knew somebody else had not just climbed out of it.

Living on an aircraft carrier took some adjusting. The six-pack sat forward, a few decks below the flight deck, under the catapults. At night, you would bolt upright from your rack when the catapults started launching 50,000-pound aircraft into the black sky blanketing the Pacific. Or when flight deck personnel tossed steel tie-down chains, used to secure the aircraft to an oft-pitching surface, onto the deck above. After a week or so, you adapted, just as I had to the freight trains that ran behind my Grandma Margaret's house in Plymouth throughout the night.

There was a lot of steel on the carrier. And a lot of ladders. The *Connie* housed more than 3,000 compartments and spaces in its 1,079-foot length and, at its widest, 270-foot beam. Her height keel to mast was seventeen stories. The only elevators were for aircraft and ordnance. I had nightmares where I was lost in the labyrinth of decks, compartments, and spaces, racing up and sliding down ladders, frantically trying to find where I needed to be. I still do on occasion.

The Navy commissioned the USS *Constellation* on October 27, 1961, five months before I was born. It cost $400 million in 1961 dollars. Four steam turbine engines, spinning four propellers twenty-one feet in diameter and weighing 44,000 pounds each, powered her. A thirty-ton, stainless steel anchor adorned each side of her bow. A single link of the 1,400-foot anchor chain weighed 360 pounds. *Connie* had over 1,300 telephones to communicate within the ship, amongst the fleet, and to the outside world. The flight deck covered over four acres of cold, unyielding steel. Internal plants distilled 400,000 gallons of fresh water and the mess crew served over 18,000 meals each and every day she was at sea.

Whether or not this interaction ever really took place, the following story still circulating on the Internet gives a poignant account of the non-lethal capabilities of a United States aircraft carrier:

> There was a conference in Europe where a number of international engineers were taking part, including European and American. During a break, one of the European engineers came back into the room saying, "Have you heard the latest dumb stunt Bush has done? He has sent an aircraft carrier to Indonesia to help the tsunami victims. What does he intend to do, bomb them?"
>
> A Boeing engineer stood up and replied quietly: "Our carriers have three hospitals on board that can treat several hundred people; they are nuclear

powered and can supply emergency electrical power to shore facilities; they have three cafeterias with the capacity to feed 5,000 people three meals a day, they can produce several hundred thousand gallons of fresh water from sea water each day, and they carry half a dozen helicopters for use in transporting victims and injured to and from their flight deck. We have eleven such ships. How many does Europe have?"

The *Connie* quietly slipped her moorings at NAS North Island in the early morning hours of December 1, embarking on a six-month deployment to the Western Pacific and Indian Oceans. She sailed out of port on only three screws (propellers) after a fuel leak led to a fire aboard ship in August, requiring round the clock repairs to meet her departure date.

Just two days out, as we steamed toward Hawaii, we were already conducting *blue-water ops*—you either land on the ship or end up in the blue water. That night, we nearly had to barricade an A-6 that kept boltering. Thankfully, on his last pass before rigging the barricade, after sucking the tanker dry, he snagged a one wire. A barricade is when you stretch a net across the flight deck and catch a twenty-ton aircraft traveling at 150 knots that way, just like coaxing a butterfly into a net in a fragrant meadow.

Forty-eight hours later, the air wing flew all night trying to locate a simulated strike force launched from Hawaii. I had LSO duty and spent much of the night on the platform catching the *birds* returning from their missions. Before sunrise on the morning of December 5, an EA-6B Prowler, crew of four, failed to return to the ship. In a postscript to a letter home started on the fourth and finished early the next day, I expressed optimism:

4 December 1988

P.S. Well, I was going to make this about how clear the night was and how many stars were out but that didn't matter when an EA-6B didn't come back to the ship this morning. We're not sure where it is and it's out of gas by now. We'll fly all night/morning on a SAR (search and rescue) and hopefully pick up a radio beacon and the crew of four in the morning. Gonna grab an hour of sleep now before the next recovery.

After writing *Good night*, I crossed out the *Good*. You would think that the E-2 radar plane was tracking the EA-6B and could locate the wreckage, and hopefully the crew, promptly. But the E-2's mission did not involve the Prowler that night. The NFOs worked air intercept control with the Tomcats and Hornets. The Pacific Ocean, the earth's largest, covers nearly sixty-four million square miles (almost a third of the earth's surface). The contiguous United States (excluding Hawaii and Alaska) covers roughly three million square miles. The air wing conducted search and rescue operations for the next three days and nights, scouring the sea for any signs of survivors or wreckage. We found none.

I attended the funeral on the hanger deck with most of the air wing and many of the ship's company. To say it was sobering to watch four empty caskets draped in American flags slide out the hanger bay doors and into the ocean does not approach the depth of feeling that swept through me. My body ached. I did not know the aircrew well but had debriefed the pilot in my capacity as an LSO. He seemed like a good guy. I felt proud of my fellow aviators and shipmates and deeply saddened by their loss—to the air wing, and, much more importantly, their families. I promised myself that I would do my best to avoid a similar fate.

As we continued plowing westward through the waves toward Hawaii, the air wing conducted a missile firing exercise on an empty frigate in the Navy's Pacific Missile Range, eighty miles off the island of Kauai. A Hornet fired the twelve-foot unarmed Harpoon missile. The air plan tasked the other aircraft, led by the E-2, with assisting the missile range in ensuring it was clear of other vessels.

The *Jag Vivek*, a 550-foot Indian freighter carrying 25,600 tons of wheat from Vancouver to Bombay, wandered into the range shortly before the exercise. When the F/A-18 pilot fired, the freighter was forty-five miles away, beyond visual range. But as the Navy press office later explained, the Hornet fired the exercise missile close enough to the *Jag Vivek*'s path for the missile's seeker to guide on it instead of the original target.

The supersonic missile tore through the living quarters located near the top of the pilot house on the stern of the ship before splashing into the ocean. We killed a thirty-six-year-old radio operator. Thankfully, the ship was still seaworthy and the damage and death we inadvertently inflicted on a foreign vessel was not worse. I was also thankful that I was a lowly lieutenant junior grade at the time and was not flying during the incident.

A two-day visit to Waikiki Beach in Hawaii a week before Christmas improved morale. I will never forget *manning the rails* as we sailed past the sunken battleship USS *Arizona* and into Pearl Harbor. A couple thousand sailors, dressed in whites, ringed the four-acre flight deck of the *Connie* at parade rest. Tear-filled eyes stared outward as we each recalled that fateful Sunday, December 7, 1941, vowing to never again let an enemy catch us unprepared.

After departing Hawaii, we continued west toward the

Philippine Islands, a group of islands in the north of the Malay Archipelago between the Pacific Ocean and the South China Sea, often referred to as the *PI* or *Philippines*. Naval Base Subic Bay, on the large northern island of Luzon, was a major ship-repair, supply, and rest and recreation facility of the Spanish Navy. It became a United States Navy base at the turn of the nineteenth century, after the Philippine-American War. The base spanned 262 square miles, about the size of Singapore. Both Subic and nearby Clark Air Force Base were severely damaged when Mount Pinatubo erupted in June 1991. Following the ill-advised closure of Subic and Clark in 1992, the Philippine government transformed the base into the Subic Bay Freeport Zone.

A letter home reflects some of the hectic monotony we all experienced in adjusting to living aboard a ship at sea and trying to stay in touch with home.

 USS CONSTELLATION CV-64

20 December 1988

Yesterday, Dec. 19, didn't happen as we crossed the international date line. I went to bed on Sunday the 18th and woke up on Tuesday the 20th. The bad thing about losing all this time on the way out is that inevitably we'll be gaining it back when we're coming home.

I got a Christmas package before Hawaii and yes, I opened the presents right away. I did however save my stocking, well most of it, and have it hanging by my rack. The chess game is great. Andy played it first on level four and it beat him. As I hate to lose and Andy is at least as good as I am, I played it last night on level three and, after a pitched battle, won. It's tough. The Rose Bowl shirt is great and I'm saving it for the game in the P.I. I think it's on at 0400 our time.

We haven't been that busy flying lately but QA has had me running around constantly. I've finally got this job whipped (almost) and once I train my new chief, I should be able to do some more reading, play some chess, work out, etc.

I took a break there to go to the LSO platform and watch a recovery. My waving day was the 19th, which we didn't have, so I went out there to get some sun and keep my eye calibrated. Speaking of the sun, it's getting awfully hot here. They say the IO will be much worse. Lots of sweating going on. Our room's air-conditioning is great though, so we sleep well.

We now have a Christmas tree with lights and lights all around the ready room. It's kind of nice, though a little depressing. All spirits are holding up though. They'd better be, as we have over five months to go. Our port calls are all holding up so far, and if we hit them all, it will be great. We pull into the PI the 30th. We will do a little flying out of Subic Bay but should have time off for liberty also.

I'm up in the tower now standing pri-fly (primary flight) duty. A pilot from each squadron involved in a launch or recovery is required to be up here with the air boss to answer any of his questions, *e.g.*, "what the hell kind of a pass was that?" Whipping boy? Scapegoat? Yes, basically, but you can also be of use if an emergency comes up.

We'll that's long over. Now I'm in the Ready Room standing an alert watch. It's 0500 and I'm tired. We stand an alert most every night as we are within range of Russian Bears now. I have watch from 0400-0600 and am here as a member of the aircrew to call the other four crewmen and the squadron duty office if the alert is called away. Then I run to the plane and we get airborne within fifteen to twenty minutes and find the bad guys.

I'll sign off now to get this in the mail. Tomorrow is our first mail (outgoing or incoming) day in a while and we may not have one for a couple of days after that. Take care and stay healthy.

Love and Happy Holidays,

Steve

P.S. Mom, I'm glad to hear you're done with chemo. I hope you're feeling well. Love you lots.

My desk job at the time was quality assurance officer. Seven enlisted men worked in the division, headed by Chief Petty Officer (CPO) Smith, a sailor with considerable experience. CPO Smith hoped to reach senior chief before retiring to his beloved Philippine Islands.

Upon taking over the assignment a year earlier, Chief Smith had explained that "chief petty officers run the Navy," but he was willing to train a wet-behind-the-ears young officer like me.

I replied: "Sure Chief Smith, that would be great. But don't forget that I write your fitness reports and am responsible for the division's performance. If you will work with me toward making the division as good as it can be, I promise to do the same and we will get along well."

We did.

AD2 David Wachter was an immense help in achieving that result. A dedicated, smart, aircraft mechanic, I would have trusted Dave with my life. In fact, I did. We all did. He, Chief Smith, and the other men in the QA division ensured that the mechanics performing the maintenance on the complex systems of the

E-2Cs we flew, executed and documented their work properly and according to prescribed procedures.

The squadron's maintenance divisions were populated with excellent young mechanics, who were also goofballs at times. Sausage came into the six-pack one evening looking incredulous.

"You guys aren't going to believe this," he began. "I step through the hatch into the space this afternoon—it's just the airmen and a petty officer—and one of the guys has his pecker hanging out of the fly of his dungarees. I ask him what the hell he's doing and he says they're playing *gazer*. This is a game they came up with where they pull their dicks out and if anybody says anything about it, they label them a dick gazer."

We laughed and shook our heads in befuddled amusement. I imagine a psychiatrist could expound at length on the homoerotic and homophobic tension on display there.

Amongst Junior's charges in the line division was Cleophus Prince Jr., a twenty-one-year-old airman. He seemed like a nice enough guy. But his shipmates caught AN Prince stealing from them during cruise. They were small items, nothing of much value, but we could not believe that a shipmate would do that. Junior went with him to Captain's Mast, after which Captain Zerr sent him to the brig. Upon our return to San Diego in June, the Navy transferred AN Prince to the brig at the 32nd Street Naval Station, where he was court-martialed in October of 1989 and processed out of the Navy.

The greater shock came when prosecutors charged AN Prince for the stalking, rape, and murder of six women in the Clairmont area of San Diego between January and September 1990. He typically scouted out their apartments and attacked as they showered. The media dubbed him the *Clairmont Killer*. He was convicted in July of 1993 and sentenced to death. Nearly thirty years later, he resides in San Quentin prison on death row, still breathing the air his six victims no longer can. Psychiatrists and others have expounded on Cleo at length.

We spent Christmas at sea. The air plan assigned Rich Elder ("Higgins," think *Magnum PI*) and me to the ready alert on December 23. The ship's radar picked up something suspicious at 2330 that night. After receiving the call to launch the alert from flight ops while asleep in our racks, we launched shortly before midnight with two Tomcats in tow to check it out. We flew west until the NFOs picked up what turned out to be a Russian Tupolev Tu-95 bomber, called a Bear, on our radar. The Bear's radar also apparently spotted us, as it turned and accelerated in our direction. The NFOs sent the Tomcats, each packing two AIM-54 Phoenix missiles, augmented by two AIM-9 Sidewinders, three AIM-7 Sparrow IIIs, and a full loadout of 20mm ammunition for their M-61 cannons, to chase it away from the battle group.

As we flew back to the carrier, I looked up at the stars illuminating a moonless sky enveloping an all-embracing ocean. I smiled as I thought of the three wise men riding their camels through the desert toward Bethlehem nearly 2,000 years ago. *The United Soviet Socialist Republic might manage to disrupt our Christmas*, I thought, *but it will not spoil it*. Rich and I flew a four-hour mission on Christmas Day and I got to bag the day trap in a smooth sea. That evening, we sat on our racks and at our desks in the six-pack sipping scotch that Blaise smuggled aboard with the mail and other supplies he flew out from the Philippines in a C-2.

In addition to the EA6-B crew, the *Connie* also lost a young sailor on Christmas Eve. Scuttlebutt (how we referred to gossip) was that he got a Dear John letter and took the plunge, but we never knew. The flight deck had no guard rails. There was the edge, a seventy-foot drop, and then the water. On Christmas Day, the carrier did *Williamson Turns*, designed to bring the ship back to the point at which the airman might have gone overboard, and the air wing flew search and rescue missions, but the vast Pacific again kept the body as its own.

3 January 1989

Dear Family,

Hi—how are you all? I really want to thank you for all the cards, magazines, and letters I've been receiving. I'm sorry it takes so much time to get a letter from or to the middle of the ocean. But it's been great to hear from you all and it's nice to know you're thinking of me, as I am of you.

We are in the Philippines now after transiting from Hawaii. We intercepted Russian Bears twice on the way here as they were locating the battle group and I was flying in the lead E-2 both times. This was really exciting, especially as both times the Bear came after us before the F-14 could join up. It is all played out as a sort of game of hide and seek. They try to find our battle group while we try to pick up their reconnaissance planes.

We pulled into NAS Cubi Point on December 30 for the *Connie* to get resupplied and have her fourth screw repaired. Navy Seabees built Cubi (Construction Unit Battalion I) during the Korean War, after civilian contractors surveyed the Zambales Mountains and surrounding jungle and said it could not be done. In just five years, the Seabees cut the mountain in half and used the soil to create a 10,000-foot-long runway and deep-water pier, capable of docking the Navy's largest aircraft carriers in Subic Bay. At a cost of one-hundred-million dollars, NAS Cubi Point involved one of the largest earthmoving projects ever undertaken, equivalent in scope to the construction of the Panama Canal.

That afternoon, Reif and Higgins took several of us to the Cubi Point officers' club for happy hour. Stepping through the door onto the garish, orange-and-purple carpeting, I took in my surroundings. Red leather stools lined the upper-level bar. Squadron plaques, dating back to the Vietnam era, covered the walls and hung from the ceiling, as they did in the bar below. After grabbing a beer, I walked past the shuffleboard table and out onto the balcony. Looking over the canopy of trees to Subic Bay, bordered by a mountainous jungle in the distance and Cubi Point airfield below, I caught my breath, thinking, *We're not in Kansas anymore.* Hearing the hum of a C-2's turboprops, I turned and watched as it approached, snapped left into the break, and entered the landing pattern at eye level. I felt like I was in the cockpit entering the pattern. Glancing down at the Red Horse lager in my left hand and cigarette in my right, instead of the yoke and throttles, I grinned.

Squadrons commissioned plaques from Filipino craftsmen to commemorate their six-month WestPac deployments. Many were simple affairs, a wooden plaque reflecting the squadron patch and the names of squadron officers. Others included elaborate carvings of aircraft, bombs, missiles, or the squadron's namesake. No matter what you commissioned, however, while generally high quality, there always seemed to be some striking flaw. For example, on the Black Eagle's plaque from my first cruise, Lt. Cdr. "Loot" Labella's name is upside down. This oddity, and the endearing quirkiness of the islands, led us to call the PI *NKR*, or not quite right. Following Subic's closure in 1992, the Navy shipped the squadron plaques and other memorabilia to the National Museum of Naval Aviation at NAS Pensacola, where it forms the decor of the Cubi Bar Café, which opened in 1996 as the museum's restaurant.

During our week in the Philippines, I got to fly both a day and a night flight with Lt. Cdr. Tomasoski. We took in the beauty of the islands from above, marveling at spectacular views of their dense emerald-green jungles, orderly crop fields, and azure waters. The crew also got to experience Olongapo, a bustling third-world city full of too many temptations for 5,000 men who had just spent Christmas and the last month at sea. I saw what Chief Smith liked about the Philippines and its wonderful people.

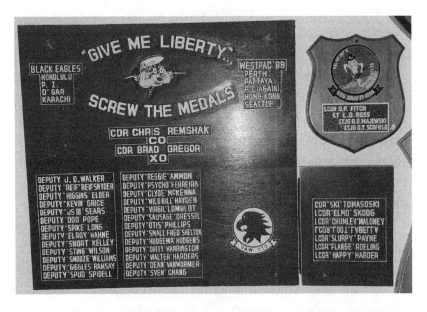

The Black Eagles' 1988-89 WestPac cruise plaque crafted in the Philippines originally hung at the NAS Cubi Point officers' club. It can be found today in the Naval Aviation Museum Restaurant in Pensacola.

Blaise, Gnarly, and Lt. Rich Payne, another VRC-50 COD pilot they lived with in the PI, gladly served as local tour guides. We rented gear and went scuba diving in Subic Bay one afternoon. After diving through murky water for about thirty minutes we spotted something bubbling up from below and swam down to check it out. It turned out to be a large diameter pipe leaking sewage into the bay. We called off the dive early and went back to their house to shower thoroughly.

We got in a round of golf at Clark Air Force base. On the eighth hole, after a solid drive that sliced a little, a long-tailed macaque monkey ran out of the jungle onto the fairway, grinned at me, and stole my ball as I approached. Unsure how to score that, I gave myself a free drop. They also took me to a few raucous bars in Olongapo, where Filipino bands did an amazing job of covering classic rock and country from the sixties and seventies. We managed to get into a barroom brawl with a group of marines one night. That was fun, except they ripped my shirt and broke Rich's rear windshield with a well-thrown whiskey bottle as, outnumbered, we escaped the altercation in his car.

USS CONSTELLATION CV-64

3 January 1989

About the PI. I met Blaise and Gnarly when we pulled in and have spent a lot of time with them. It's good to have local tour guides. The Philippines is an extremely beautiful country with lush jungles and green mountains. However, the downtown Olongapo area makes Detroit look like La Jolla. The level of poverty is amazing but the people, who have probably never known anything else, don't seem to mind. Though there are a lot of street hustlers, pick pockets, etc. I've also met a lot of very nice, honest, and hardworking Filipinos. The prices aren't as great as we were hoping for and a lot of stuff, especially electronics, is just as expensive and in some cases more expensive than back home. They do a lot of good woodworking though and it is impressive and inexpensive. They can copy anything. You just give them a picture of something and they make it for you.

> They have bands out in town that copy American music quite well also. It's pretty funny to be listening to somebody who sounds just like Willie Nelson and look up to see a Filipino band.

We departed the Philippines four days later than scheduled, on January 9, 1989. We delayed to conserve diesel fuel marine (DFM). The *Connie* and other ships in Battle Group Delta burned a lot. The delay meant we would skip our planned port call in Singapore.

I often complained in my letters home about our sporadic operating schedule in efforts to save DFM and JP-5 (what the planes burned). As I wrote home on January 3, 1989:

 USS CONSTELLATION CV-64

> It seems to me if they're going to spend a year getting us ready for this and send us out here for six months they could at least pay for our gas. I guess I shouldn't complain though, as it bodes well on the world situation that there seems to be not that much for us to do out here.

After pulling out of the PI, I flew once in four days, followed by an all-night alert and two four-hour flights the next day. As I complained in another letter home: *Sometimes I think the people in Operations use a dart board to put us on the flight schedule.* You learned to catch an hour of sleep here and there during the day so you could stay up all night when necessary. We had a saying about living on the ship: "You get eight hours of sleep at night and whatever you get during the day is gravy." The problem, eight hours at night was often just one or two.

In mid-January we passed through the Malaccan Straight

between Malaysia and Sumatra. We sailed past Singapore at the southern tip of Malaysia, longingly looking at it from the ship, wishing that our Carrier Group Commander, Rear Admiral Ken Carlsen, had not cancelled our port call. After transiting the straight, we got back on a more regular flight schedule as we set out to spend the next two-and-a-half months in the Indian Ocean.

CHAPTER 9

GONZO STATION

THE CONNIE AND THE REST of Battle Group Delta relieved the the USS Nimitz, CVN-68,[1] of responsibility for the Gulf of Oman Naval Zone of Operations (GONZO) on January 17. The United States designated Gonzo Station as an area of carrier-based naval operations by the Navy and Marine Corps in the northern Indian Ocean and Arabian Sea during the 1979-1981 Iranian Hostage Crisis. After arriving on station, the air wing conducted surface search control (looking for Soviet or other enemy ships)

---

[1] The N denotes that the *Nimitz* was nuclear powered. The *Connie* was conventionally powered. All current US aircraft carriers and many other navy ships are nuclear powered. US nuclear powered warships have safely operated for more than fifty years without experiencing any reactor accident or any release of radioactivity that hurt human health or had an adverse effect on marine life. Naval reactors have an outstanding record of over 134 million miles safely steamed on nuclear power, and they have amassed over 5,700 reactor-years of safe operation. Ryan White, "How Safe [are] the U.S. Nuclear Powered Warships?" Naval Post (March 17, 2021), https://navalpost.com/how-safe-the-u-s-nuclear-powered-warships/.
I do not foresee warships or warplanes operating via solar panels, windmills, or batteries in any of our lifetimes. I highly recommend Michael Shellenberger's excellent book *Apocalypse Never: Why Environmental Alarmism Hurts Us All* if you are interested in a cogent explanation about energy density and our misguided efforts to save the planet and its people from climate change. Bjorn Lomborg's *False Alarm, How Climate Change Panic Costs Us Trillions, Hurts the Poor, and Fails to Fix the Planet* is another well-written, informative book on the topic.

and air intercept control (looking for unidentified planes and sending fighters to intercept them) missions.

The ship implemented no-fly days on Sundays, an unwelcome development:

USS CONSTELLATION CV-64

23 January 1989

I'm afraid this will provide a routine. We'll start to know and care what day of the week it is and time will start to drag. As of now, I couldn't tell you if it's Tuesday or Saturday without looking at a calendar.

Cdr. Remshak certified me, Junior, Sausage, Spike, and Otis as CAPCs on the twenty-fifth. The certification letter stated: "In your performance as a carrier aircraft plane commander, you must be constantly aware of your responsibilities and assure yourself that every measure is taken to ensure the safety of your aircraft and aircrew."

At age twenty-six, my job (one of them) was to pilot a $90 million aircraft off a catapult, fly a four-hour mission in the United States' cold war against its adversaries, and then land that aircraft and its crew of five safely back aboard the aircraft carrier in any and all-weather conditions. I did it to the best of my ability and with immense pride.

Once launched from the ship, the E-2 flew out a hundred miles or so and set up station. It then flew circles for the next few hours. We called it *drilling holes in the sky*. The E-2 had longer legs (burned less fuel and could thus fly longer) than the jets it flew with. As a result, E-2 missions often covered two and sometimes three, one-and-a-half-hour flight cycles. The NFOs were busy for those hours, the pilots not so much. Other than monitor radios and instruments, there was not much for the pilots to do during the often four-and-a-half-hour flights on cruise. Sausage and I would play chess on a small magnetic board when flying together. I once had to write up a gripe (aircraft maintenance request) admitting: "black pawn lost in cockpit." The maintenance crew was not pleased and let us know it. Reif brought an astronomy book on cruise. During night flights we would identify constellations in the limitless and often otherwise lightless sky.

We had a minor mishap when our carrier air group commander (CAG) Capt. W.S. "Bud" Orr, an attack pilot in the Vietnam War who flew over one hundred combat missions and won numerous air medals, left the parking brake on in an F-14 when he launched off the catapult. Both tires blew, of course. But he flew a flawless approach to a safe trap and took the ribbing—such as captain in charge of the air wing gets—well.

After about a month in the Indian Ocean, the *Connie's* skipper, Captain John J. Zerr, cancelled flight ops and ordered a steel beach picnic. The sun blazed at four degrees latitude. The ship's crew threw frisbees, footballs, and baseballs around the flight deck, until an errant throw or missed catch sent the disc or ball over the side and into the ocean. Shipmates hit golf balls and shot skeet off the fantail. I listened to some surprisingly good musical sets; rednecks from flyover country can jam. We all ate steaks, barbecue chicken, burgers, and hot dogs, enjoying our time tanning in the sun—at least the 90 percent or so who were not on watch. Breaks like that broke up the monotony of working around the clock for weeks on end. The grind, even when broken up by the thrill of flying on and off the carrier, wore on you.

In early February we conducted a Weapons Week on the way to Diego Garcia. Aircraft ordnance personnel loaded the Tomcats with Phoenix, Sparrow, and Sidewinder missiles. The Hornets carried Sparrow, Sidewinder, and Harpoon missiles, as well as laser-guided and other bombs to complement their M61A1 Vulcan

20mm cannon. Intruders each carried a full load of twenty-eight MK-82 500-pound bombs.[2] As much as we enjoyed conducting simulated strikes, we all looked forward to setting foot on land for the first time in weeks when we got to Diego.

Diego Garcia is a militarized atoll just south of the equator in the central Indian Ocean. The atoll is located 2,197 miles east of Tanzania, 1,116 miles south-southwest of the southern tip of India, and 2,935 miles west-northwest of the west coast of Australia. Diego Garcia lies at the southernmost tip of the Chagos-Laccadive Ridge, an underwater mountain range with peaks consisting of coral reefs, atolls, and islands comprising Lakshadweep, the Maldives, and the Chagos Archipelago. I would be aboard the USS *Independence* a year and a half later about to fly into Diego for some rest and relaxation leave (R&R) when Iraq would invade Kuwait and change our plans.

One of the scariest and most difficult landings of my career was not trying to get aboard the carrier on the edge of a hurricane at night (which occurred six weeks later off the coast of Australia) but flying into Diego Garcia on February 10, 1989. I could not blame it on the *Connie's* navigator, who seemed to put the carrier in rainstorms on purpose during flight ops, when towering cumulonimbus clouds built up over the island and thunderstorms engulfed it while we flew our mission. It was only my second flight as CAPC. Otis rode in the right seat. The skipper, as mission commander, sat in the center seat in *the tube,* as we called the narrow tunnel the NFOs

---

[2]   The Navy's all weather, deep strike bomber, the A-6 Intruder, like the E-2, was an unattractive but remarkably capable aircraft. During the Intruder's heyday, it was second only to the Air Force's B-52 in payload. Yet the A-6 was only fifty-four feet long, with a fifty-three-foot wingspan. The B-52 is 159 feet long by 185 feet wide. More importantly, while a B-52 takes a two-mile long runway to lug its payload aloft, an Intruder went from 0-150 kts and was on its way with its massive payload after a 300-foot catapult shot.

sat sideways in while operating their radar scopes during flight. The mission went well, and the flight plan called for us to land on Diego Garcia and spend the night there. The ship would dock at Diego's deep-water port the next day.

Diego had an airport tower and a radio beacon, but no radar facilities. There was a single runway on the narrow end of the island. More than a dozen planes from the mission we had just wrapped were all low on fuel and heading into Diego to land. As I mentioned earlier, flying in thunderstorms is not something you do if you do not have to. We all had to. None of us had enough fuel to get back to the carrier and there was no tanker. The E-2 did not have a refueling probe anyway, although Grumman added one in 2016. It was Diego or ditch.

The idea of us all trying to get to a runway where we could not see each other and there was no radar to keep us separated as we bounced through the turbulence caused some concern. To keep things safe, such as we could, we stayed back while the NFOs sequenced the other planes into the runway with our radar as we ran lower on fuel, the clouds descended, and the storm intensified. That task accomplished, it was our turn to land.

We danced between the clouds using VFR (visual flight rules) until we got about thirty miles from the island and went into *the goo*, as pilots called the clouds. I switched to IFR (instrument flight rules). As we blindly closed on the tower beacon, I told Otis, "we have to try to get below these clouds" and started to descend. Otis called "watch your altitude," as we passed 1,000 feet with a healthy rate of descent. I pulled back on the yoke to level off.

We broke through the clouds at 800 feet, the hangars of the airfield appearing large and close below.

I radioed the tower: "Hawkeye six-oh-two, field in sight."

The controller in the tower responded, "Hawkeye six-oh-two, you are cleared to land, any runway, at your own risk."

Thanks for the vote of confidence, I thought. Cleared to land, any runway at a one runway airport like Diego meant we could land heading in either direction. The tower did not care or think it mattered which. It also clearly wanted no responsibility.

The winds blew in swirling gusts and the rain came down as if the heavens were emptying bathtubs onto our windscreen. The wipers worked furiously, but ineffectively as I managed to line the plane up with the flooded runway. Dropping the left wing fifteen degrees and keeping at least forty pounds of pressure on the right rudder, I put the plane in a side slip to compensate for the crosswind and keep aligned with the runway centerline.

Noting what appeared to be Class III rapids flowing across the pavement, Otis calmly commented, "That's a lot of water." I agreed and planted the plane hard on landing to reduce hydroplaning. Keeping my feet off the brakes, I carefully pulled the throttles all the way back to full reverse thrust. We slowed without skidding off into the grass and my heart rate got back down into a safer zone by the time we cleared the runway and taxied to the hangar.

The skipper bought the crew beers at the officers' club that evening. The next morning the carrier pulled in. The plan of the day on the *Footprint of Freedom*, as we referred to Diego Garcia due to its narrow shape and large lagoon in the center, included swimming, diving, snorkeling, and volleyball. That evening, the air wing threw a party at the officers' club and blew off some steam from the previous month at sea. As I wrote home: *the damage to the club was only in the three-figure range, so all-in-all, it was a good night.* After spending the next morning relaxing at the beach, Otis and I flew the bird and crew back to the boat. Several lucky members of the *Connie's* crew got assigned to a Diego beach detachment, returning to the ship weeks later tanned, relaxed, and refreshed.

A full flight schedule filled the rest of February. One thing that broke up the tedium was the opportunity to train to fly the E-2 in the air demonstration the air wing planned to fly for dignitaries from Pakistan. Lt. Cdr. Rich Payne flew in the left seat, but I got to ride shotgun. All we did was a low flyby at 200 feet and pop up next to the ship, but the F-14s did a fly by at Mach (breaking the sound barrier) and the F/A-18s and A-6s fired their cannons on strafing runs and dropped bombs.

On February 28, the day before we pulled into Karachi, Pakistan, the US Ambassador, Robert Oakley, and Prime Minister Benazir Bhutto's husband, Asif Zardari, flew out to the *Connie* with other dignitaries in the COD. They toured the ship and then the air wing put on the air demo. All went well until the A-6s dropped their bombs a half mile off the port side of the carrier. A piece of shrapnel somehow made it all the way back to the flight deck and punctured the radome of one of our Hawkeyes. It is hard to be the eyes and ears of the fleet without a radar. It is nearly as hard to get a twenty-four-foot diameter radome out to the Indian Ocean to replace one with a hole in it. The other unfortunate event at that ill-fated airshow was when the bombs took out a pod of dolphins, which was definitely in the wrong place at the wrong time in that enormous ocean.

We spent three days in Karachi, which was enough. It was a dirty, impoverished city and the people were sullen. A street hustler offered me heroin when I went ashore. I settled for a ride on a camel and never really did get the smell out of my jeans. I went shopping and purchased a camel skin jacket that I still wear today, onyx chess set, and set of six stone glasses for a hundred US dollars. We spent more buying an illegal case of beer through the Sheraton Karachi. Pakistan is a dry country in many ways. About twenty of us shared a suite at the Sheraton and I slept on the top shelf of the closet the first night. I did not sleep well, but no drunken sailors tripped over or fell onto me.

My complaints about the flight schedule came back to haunt me when Spud assumed responsibility for the Quality Assurance Division and I moved to the Operations Department. I took over writing the flight schedule from Rush Williams ("Snooze," due to his laid-back manner). Once I was responsible for writing the squadron flight schedule, I complained that the ship's Air Operations Department did not get me the overall air plan by 1800 like they were supposed to. This required me to work out our flight schedule, which had to conform to the overall air plan, late into most evenings, or later if I was flying or waving that night.

When you did have down time aboard ship, napping was always the first choice. Otherwise, you worked out in a small weight room that was aft, just off the engine room and thus a bit of a workout and a steam at the same time, watched movies on a VCR in the ready room, wrote home, read, or played cards or chess. It took a while, but once Blaise joined us for the Indian Ocean portion of cruise, flying supplies, mail, and an occasional bottle of scotch in and out of Diego, we had enough for a decent poker game. I touted my poker prowess to Mom and Dad: *I guess Grandma Margaret taught me well, as I am up about $130 after the first two games.*

Letters were an important part of cruise, keeping you grounded in what you were doing and for whom. While in the middle of the Indian Ocean, it could take a month for a letter to get home and then a response to arrive back to the ship. That was a long time to wait to hear from family and friends. Email and cell phones were not yet invented, and long-distance phone calls from overseas were prohibitively expensive. Thus, letters served as the primary and often only method of communication with the outside world. Further, the classified nature of the carrier's whereabouts, operations, and planned destinations limited what we could tell our loved ones about where we were and what we were doing.

At times, the isolation and loneliness of being aboard ship, hundreds of miles from land, depressed my spirits. Other times, the daily navigation of 5,000 other bodies built a desperate desire for the solitude I both craved and loathed. When these emotions collided, often in the middle of the night, sleep evaded me. I would quietly slide out of my rack and take a restless walk along the moonlit edges of the flight deck or climb the tower to search the enigmatic ocean for answers. *No joy*, a pilot's acknowledgment that he could not locate what he was trying to find. Always lonely, but never alone.

Despite high-quality maintenance, the Hawkeyes we flew were old and did break on occasion. One day, while taxiing up to the catapult, the plane's hydraulic system warning light illuminated. I unstrapped and ran back to check the reservoir. It was empty and the floor of the aircraft was soaked in sticky, red hydraulic fluid. We aborted the mission. I got lucky in two respects that day:

USS CONSTELLATION CV-64

19 February 1989
It's ironic that we weren't airborne. Usually, we are launched first but today two planes got off ahead of us, allowing us to catch the problem before launch. We have a back-up system, so we could have gotten safely back aboard but it's certainly better to catch something like that on the deck. The second good thing is that I am no longer QAO, so the report is Spud's problem.

My most terrifying landing of cruise occurred off the western coast of Australia. The air plan had us doing air intercept control at night. We launched in the rain, and the weather got worse during the mission. We flew in the goo on instruments all night. After wrapping the mission, we marshalled with the other aircraft stacked in a holding pattern ten miles aft of the carrier awaiting the call down for approach. A hurricane to the south caused towering swells and whitecaps to buffet the carrier as it steamed into the wind at top speed.

Spike and I listened to the radio as multiple planes boltered or the LSOs waved them off the pitching flight deck due to unsafe conditions. Later, I learned that the deck was maxing out its pitch meter, moving more than forty vertical feet as it rose and fell in the swells. The mission had been long, nearly four hours of flight time, and we were tired. We just wanted to get aboard, grab a bite to eat, and get to sleep. Upon getting the call-down from approach, I held the yoke in a death grip, but gently, as I focused singularly on flying the best instrument approach of my life.

I employed two training lessons toward that end. The first involved maintaining a rapid, but thorough, scan. You monitored many instruments when flying—airspeed, altitude, heading, hydraulic pressure, oil temperature and pressure, and more. A good scan checked each every few seconds, while also maintaining a view outside when VFR. For an IFR approach you *flew the needles* that indicated lineup and glideslope as you closed on the carrier. In an approach like that night's, with gusts striking violently and randomly, you skipped scanning hydraulic and oil pressure, and did your best to fly the needles while maintaining airspeed and angle of attack.

The second lesson was compartmentalization. You may recall the scene early in the movie *Top Gun* where Cougar loses his nerve after an encounter with two Russian MiGs. He is flying a very shaky approach, looking at a picture of his wife and child he has affixed to his instrument panel, when Maverick pulls up beside him to help get him aboard. After surviving the landing, Cougar goes to his commanding officer and turns in his wings. He tells his CO, "I am holding on too tight," opening a slot for Maverick and Goose in the Navy Fighter Weapons School.

Proper compartmentalization would never allow that to

happen. Thoughts of family, friends, and home were great—they were why we were in the Indian Ocean trying to land a plane on a boat in a thunderstorm at the edge of a hurricane. But you must banish such thoughts when focus is paramount. Thus, you trained yourself to put them in a compartment at the back of your mind and lock them in there until you and your crew were safe. Only then could you open the compartment and pull them out again. You did *not* think about your wife, girlfriend, mother, or dog when the situation required your concentration elsewhere, else you might never see them again.

The needles were spot on when we broke out of the clouds at 200 feet and saw the carrier looming large less than an eighth of a mile away. The red drop-down lights on the fantail were gyrating like Spike and I had never seen before. I called "Hawkeye ball." Just then, Spike announced, "I can see the screws" as *Connie's* massive propellers breached the surface of the raging ocean. Heeding the LSO's call to "come left," we slammed into the bucking flight deck, snagging a two wire.

After parking and dropping off my flight gear, I postponed my snack and rack, threw on my white flotation safety vest, and raced out to the LSO platform. I watched in pelting rain as the rest of the planes struggled to get aboard. Eventually, everyone made it back safely, although several jets had to refuel in flight before they did. The duty LSO gave me an <u>OK</u> for the pass I flew. We also got a call from CAG Orr, who congratulated us on getting aboard in some of the worst conditions he had ever seen. I could not have been prouder.

We spent Easter at sea. I attended a non-denominational service in the bow. We prayed for the safety of our shipmates, our country, ourselves, and our world between the ship's two, massive anchor chains.

Sailors lowered one of the two 60,000-pound anchors that hung from those chains off the coast of Perth on Friday morning,

March 31. In my view, Perth took the gold for the best port visit of cruise, beating out Pattaya Beach, Thailand, and Hong Kong, which took the silver and bronze, respectively. I watched as shipmates began piling onto liberty boats the Australians provided to take them ashore. I had pulled an aircraft integrity watch from 0800 to 1200, and then picket boat officer duty from 2000 to 2400. Aircrew served as watch officers for the ship, along with their other duties. We all worked together. I looked ashore impatiently as I patrolled the massive warship, ensuring that no radical Western Australians tried to board and defile her by taking over the flight deck and throwing some *shrimp on the barbie.*

The ship cancelled the picket boat—a thirty-five-foot watercraft that patrolled the perimeter of the carrier while anchored—at 2300. The Australians did not appear to be hostile. After donning a pair of whites (the *ice cream man suit,* as we called the uniform), I caught the next liberty boat ashore at 2330. The battle group party was over, so I grabbed a cab to the Hilton, where the squadron rented a suite and Junior, Spike, Mike Wilson ("Sting" based on his resemblance to the lead singer of the Police), and I were sharing a room. We spent Saturday day at the mall and night at the casino. On Sunday VF/A-25, the Fist of the Fleet, threw a party and we stopped by. Reif, John Sears, and I met three lovely Australian girls there who took us to a club by the beach.

The Black Eagles hosted a party Tuesday night. We went all out. The squadron mimeographed flyers and handed them out to pretty lasses and other fun-looking folks all over Perth. We put together a play list of solid music, ordered kegs and liquor, and, critically, insisted that the Perth Hilton set up a stage in the large Swan Room we reserved for the event.

As Reif explained: "The key to a great party is killer music and a stage, preferably for the live band, but if that's not an option you still need a platform to engage the crowd from and keep the energy level up."

In matters of party planning—really partying in general—Reif was the Oracle at Delphi, assisted by eager sorcerer's apprentices like myself.

Some 350 partygoers stopped by and nearly all stayed. We danced, drank, and sang boisterously from the stage with our newfound mates until the Hilton shut us down at 0200. Wednesday started late and ended early with a delicious Italian dinner. On Thursday, Cherone, Linda, and Penny—the girls we met at the VF/A-25 party—invited Reif, John, and me to Kings Peak for a picnic. Later, we went to the observation point on the beach and grabbed a beer at the pier before boarding the last liberty boat back to the *Connie* right before our midnight curfew. It was a much-needed break at the two-thirds point of the cruise— reminding us of what we were out here risking our lives for—a way of life rooted in liberty and freedom that the Aussies shared.

CHAPTER 10

TRANSITING HOME

WE PULLED ANCHOR AND STEAMED out of Perth on April 7. The USS *Ranger*, CV-61, relieved the *Connie* of Indian Ocean responsibilities shortly thereafter. After being relieved, we embarked on a fun, port-filled transit east, exceedingly thankful to be heading home.

We had lost five men and a plane, and accidentally killed a foreign sailor and a pod of dolphins. But by projecting American power in support of freedom, we had stifled the advances of totalitarian adversaries like the Soviet Union. A military and economic superpower like the United States is obligated to defend liberty and enforce international norms around the globe. Seeing a carrier battle group sailing in nearby waters tends to remind those countries and despots that would do harm to the United States or its allies of our strength and resolve, and to dissuade them from bad behavior.

Heading home we crossed the international date line for the second time, enduring a do-over day as penance for the one we skipped on the way out.

I flew my only bolter on that cruise on April 9, 1989. A bright blue sky unblemished by clouds surrounded the carrier as it sailed on an uncharacteristically calm ocean. The pristine conditions lulled me into losing focus in the final seconds. I added too much power to correct for a sinking ball and touched down beyond the four wire. To make matters worse, Spike was in the right seat and CAPC on the flight. He just shook his head twice and then dropped it forward from his shoulders as we got airborne again, not disguising his disgust.

The only people that hate bolters as much as the pilot that flies one—and the air boss, LSOs, and your copilot—are the NFOs in the back. Pilots fondly refer to E-2 NFOs as *moles* due to their dark, tunnel-like workspace. Upon feeling the crash into the flight deck, but not the decelerating jerk of an arresting cable, the NFOs realize they must trust their lives to you once again, hoping you do not mess up any worse than you just did.

Spike never boltered. He would rather get a no grade for slamming the plane into the flight deck than take the crew around the pattern for another go. I know this because as an LSO I gave him one once when he did.

His response, when I told him: "Spike, when you go that high, you have to take the bolter."

"Fuck you, McKenna. I got aboard, didn't I?"

We flew together again that night after my bolter, and I regained a little pride by bagging an OK three wire on a cloudy, moonless night.

The Crossing the Line Ceremony was a rite of passage held when a ship, military or civilian, crossed the equator. We skipped the ceremony on the way out, knowing we could observe it when heading home. Sailors who had previously undergone the traditional hazing before crawling to the Tank of Truth and Wisdom, a salt-water bath that transformed slimy pollywogs into trusty shellbacks, looked forward to the day with fiendish anticipation. Us slimy wogs—not so much.

More than fifty sailors competed in a beauty contest on Sunday night to get the festivities rolling. The judges included Admiral Carlsen, Captains Zerr, McHenry, Schmidt, and Orr, and the *Connie's* XO, Commander Shean. They voted to crown OSSN Jones from the Operations Department as wog princess and appointed four royal handmaidens to serve in his, or her, court.

Trusty shellbacks roused us slimy wogs at 0500 on Monday, April 12 and herded us to the mess deck. Once there, they served us a concoction of coffee grounds, sour milk, and pepper sauce. After breakfast, shellbacks made us crawl around on our hands and knees on the floor covered in mess-deck garbage: eggs, butter, and rotted vegetables. They then led the wogs—officer and enlisted alike—to the flight deck.

Shellbacks pelted us with sardines, tomato sauce, week-old creole spaghetti, and green oysters, whacked us with shillelaghs, and blasted us with fire hoses as we crawled over the hot, rough, steel deck. Next came a tunnel filled with more garbage that we slithered through on our way to the Tank of Truth and Wisdom. Shellbacks forced wogs to kiss the feet of the wog princess, or the sardine-smeared navel of the royal baby (the fattest chief petty officer). Kangaroo courts were empaneled and sentenced wogs to time in the stocks or, morbidly, to be crammed into a giant coffin, for some trumped up transgression or another. I avoided those humiliations and, upon washing off the tomato sauce and oysters in the salt-water bath, emerged a duly initiated member of the Order of the Trusty Shellback.

Rites of passage have existed throughout history. Ancient Romans are reported to have brought boys to the public forum when they reached the age of fourteen. Once there, the boys exchanged their childhood clothes and bulla (a protective amulet received nine days after birth) for a toga and a public first shave as they became Roman citizens. Roman girls transitioned even earlier, at twelve, when they were pledged to be married and led to the temple of Artemis. Once there, they proved their womanhood by giving up all their childhood toys.

If that sounds harsh, the Nootka natives of the Vancouver Islands routinely hurled menstruating girls into the Pacific. As soon a girl got her first period, female elders would take her out to sea in a boat and throw her overboard, naked. If the girl had enough strength to make it back to shore without becoming the main course at a feeding frenzy, a great celebration ensued, completing her transition to womanhood.

Such rites of passage have a purpose. No one should ever haze those that cannot handle it (or throw menstruating young girls into a frigid, shark-infested ocean to swim ashore) but a rite of passage is a profound thing that should not be taken lightly. At its best, it culls the unsuited and instills camaraderie amongst the initiated. At its worst, it persecutes and ridicules the weak. As with most things, balance is key.

We anchored off Pattaya Beach, Thailand on April 17. Pattaya Beach was enchanting, but no Perth. Instead of clean, roomy liberty boats to carry us ashore, we boarded narrow fishing boats, shoulder to shoulder, for the thirty-minute transit. *I could probably swim ashore faster,* I thought, longing to set foot on dry land and eagerly anticipating the awaiting adventures. The hotel resort we stayed in had a pool, one of those giant chessboards with two-and-a-half-foot tall pieces, and a small elephant chained up in the back (which was cruel). With a healthy bank account after five months at sea, I no longer needed to sleep on a closet shelf or share a queen-size bed.

After joining in the Thai's raucous celebration of their New Year on April 19, mainly by being the targets of their squirt guns and water balloons on the streets of Pattaya, several shipmates and I enjoyed a memorable meal on the beach. At sunset, we sat down to long tables laden with all sorts of delicious seafood—lobster, crab, giant prawns and shrimp, grouper, yellowtail, and cobia, along with buckets full of steamed mussels and clams. Sautéed vegetables, freshly baked bread, and endless pitchers of strong beer surrounded the sumptuous seafood. It was a feast worthy of Bangkok royalty and cost ten dollars.

From Thailand we sailed back to Subic Bay and spent the last week of April there. We visited Hong Kong next, arriving on May 4. Hong Kong, the city where East meets West, was amazing. I am afraid that is no longer true now, just twenty-five years after the United Kingdom turned it over to Communist China on July 1, 1997. China recently reneged on its promise to grant Hong Kong autonomy until 2047. Mainland China, ruled with a beguiling smile and an iron fist by the leader of the Chinese Communist Party, Xi Xiaoping, now arrests and persecutes political opponents in Hong Kong with impunity. Chairman Xi also appears poised to annex the twenty-four-million people of Taiwan, assuming the rest of the world offers no resistance or aid to the freedom-loving people of Taiwan either.

Buying a custom-made suit in Kowloon, the most populous urban area in Hong Kong, was a highlight. The tailors of Hong Kong rivaled those on Savoy Row in London. Exquisite craftsmen working with top quality fabrics. The process began with a visit to the shop, where they served you beer and upsold you on fine wool, stitching, monogramed shirts, etc. The measurement process reminded me of my NAMI physical at AOCS. After that you paid and scheduled a fitting for the next day. The Hong Kong tailors must have worked all night when a 5,000-person carrier visited. The finished product arrived a month or so after we got home. It fit splendidly and did not disappoint.

But the squadron dinner at the American Club topped the suit. The American Club was, and last I heard remains, the premier, private business and social club in Hong Kong. The views from its large glass windows overlooked the straight between Hong Kong and Kowloon to the north and Hong Kong Harbor to the east. I have never seen a busier or more eclectic port, teeming with everything from oil tankers larger than an aircraft carrier to small sampans and junks, traversing the harbor like ants in an ant farm.

All the squadron officers attended, save a couple that had duty on the ship. We feasted on steak and seafood, cooked to perfection and washed down with copious amounts of wine. Sated after a sumptuous meal, I ordered a round of cognac for all my fellow officers, aviators, warriors, and friends. When my bill for that extravagance arrived, I realized I had spent a month's worth of flight pay on a round of drinks. I was okay with that.

As much as we enjoyed Hong Kong, by that point we all longed for home. First, however, the admiral tasked us with playing cat and mouse once again with the USSR's Air Force and Navy. This time we sparred in the Aleutian Island Chain extending off Alaska toward our Cold War foe's Kamchatka Peninsula. The Aleutians separate the Pacific Ocean from the Bering Sea to the north. The weather in the Pacific above fifty degrees latitude is stormy in May. The water temperature is also around fifty degrees, meaning even in a dry suit (which we had to wear when flying, or trying to sleep when on the ready alert) you would succumb to hypothermia within an hour or two. The Navy issued a table that told you how long you had, based on water and air temperature. I saw no point in studying that too closely.

The ship's Operations Department wanted an approach the air wing could fly to the carrier while it was hiding between islands in the Aleutian Chain. It assigned me the task of designing one. I devised an approach that pilots could fly safely, but the clustered and mountainous islands did not make it easy. The consequences of straying from the approach by as little as a thousand feet horizontally, or a hundred feet vertically were fatal, however, and CAG Orr wisely nixed the plan. I did get to work with the ship's Operations Department and spend time in the CIC (combat information center) though—an eye-opening experience. Giant, transparent screens tracked the aircraft around the carrier, the other ships in the battle group, and, when present, USSR or other countries' aircraft and ships. I found the focus and intensity of the officers and enlisted personnel working in the CIC mesmerizing and reassuring.

The carrier's closed-circuit TV system had monitors in all the ready rooms and many other common spaces. The ship had taped and broadcast a recording where I explained my overly dangerous approach procedure to the air wing. It was not a hit. Captain's Mast was much more popular.

On a Navy ship, or any other, the captain was in complete control. There is often no time for debate at sea, especially in combat. The captain of the aircraft carrier was accountable to the admiral but had full authority to maintain order on his ship as he saw fit. Capt. Zerr held Captain's Mast once a week. Picture the *People's Court* or *Judge Judy* at sea. Sailors that missed or fell asleep on a watch or committed some other offense were given a chance to plead their case before the captain. Capt. Zerr punished small infractions with a stern admonition and extra duty or a fine. Other offenses, however, could be quite ingenious, and disgusting. One young sailor, after receiving discipline from a chief petty officer the day before, urinated in the chiefs' coffee urn before delivering it the next morning. He got a week in the brig on bread and water. Another smuggled aboard a prostitute from the Philippines and stowed her away in the bow until she was discovered and returned home. Skipper Zerr threw that criminal in the brig until having him flown off the ship for prosecution. While most offenses were minor, maintaining discipline on a warship (that may or may not carry nuclear weapons) is crucial. Even minor infractions that impact the safety of the ship or its crew must be punished and not be repeated. Capt. Zerr meted out punishment swiftly, fairly, and effectively. And it also made entertaining TV viewing for the crew.

Toward the end of our stay in the Northern Pacific, Otis and I, cocooned in the cockpit wearing our dry suits and flight gear, witnessed a storm engulf the carrier and send its deck pitching nearly like it had off Australia. Spike was flying another E-2 at the time and the first plane the carrier recovered. After observing that landing, which Spike flew expertly but still nearly crashed, CAG Orr directed the remaining aircraft flying at the time to divert to Shemya Island.

Shemya is a tiny, two-by-four-mile island toward the western end of the Aleutian Island chain. It sits 200 miles east of Russia and 1,200 miles southwest of Anchorage. A US Air Force radar, surveillance, weather, and aircraft refueling station, including a 10,000-foot-long runway, opened on Shemya in 1943 and is still in operation. Air traffic control and radar facilities we could have used in Diego Garcia made landing on the island uneventful, albeit in a driving rain and wicked crosswind.

After tying down the aircraft, we waited in the base of the tower until 1400 to see if the weather would clear. It did not, so we went to the officers' club. As the only bar on base, frequent patrons included enlisted Air Force personnel—no need to get too concerned with rank on an island at the end of the Aleutians.

The next day we sat in the BOQ until the carrier radioed at noon that the weather would again preclude take off. We felt impotent and vulnerable, stranded on an island so close to the USSR. Frigid winds blew across the single runway at a steady twenty-five to thirty knots, with gusts clocking in much higher. You could land in winds like that, but if you tried to take off, they would blow the aircraft off the runway before you could get up the speed to counter them and get airborne. A log, six inches in diameter, hanging from a chain, served as the airfield windsock. It fluttered around at a thirty-degree angle throughout the day as we watched from the officers' club bar. I suspect that spending too much time on Shemya is bad for your liver.

The weather cleared on May 20, allowing us to depart the island. It was one of the only times I looked forward to getting back to living aboard ship—mainly because we were only ten days and a *wake-up* from home. CPO Smith taught me how to count the days until you got home; something you did frequently on a six-month deployment. You started count the day we pulled out of port, at 181. To get to the fewest number of days remaining at sea, you did not count the present day or the day you got home. The day you were already in did not count because you were already in it. The day you got home, you only woke up aboard ship, you got to sleep elsewhere, so it did not count either.

CHAPTER 11

TIGER CRUISE

THE *CONNIE* PULLED INTO SEATTLE on May 26. Various family members flew in to greet their husbands, sons, brothers, and fathers, including my mom and dad, my younger sister Sarah, and Aunt Edie. They, along with various other parents, took several of us out to a fancy restaurant that night and listened with appropriate pride as we recounted our exploits overseas.

When we pulled out of Seattle the next day, my dad, along with Spike's and Otis's, assumed Junior, Spud, and Sausage's bunks in the six-pack while they flew home to their families several days early. The *Connie* welcomed more than 1,100 fathers, sons, relatives, and friends, better known as *Tigers*, aboard for the five-day sail from Seattle to San Diego.

The Tigers enjoyed watching flight operations and other demonstrations of the aircraft carrier's weaponry on the short cruise home. The ship impressed us all when it fired the Phalanx CIWS (close-in weapon system). The CIWS was a radar-guided 20mm Vulcan canon mounted on a swiveling base. It fired 3,000 rounds a minute (fifty a second) in short bursts with a "Pffffft," and could obliterate any small ship, missile, or other threat approaching the carrier.

Spike, Otis, and I all had solid sea legs at that point and knew the ship well—although many of her 3,000 spaces remained unexplored even after half a year. We gave our dads tours of the ready room, hangar, engine room, flight deck, and other spaces that did not require a security clearance. They lived like us, eating meals in the mess hall, sleeping in a bunk slightly narrower than a twin sized bed, and taking lukewarm showers (both my WestPac cruises were on conventional, oil-powered carriers, and with energy at a premium, the ship did not waste much on hot showers). I even took our dads out to the LSO platform to watch a recovery.

One downside of having our dads on the ship—Spike, Otis, and I were initially taken off the flight schedule. The last thing the air wing wanted was for a father to watch his son kill himself and his crew, while destroying a multi-million-dollar aircraft in the process. Nonsense. After over five months flying on and off the carrier, we knew the aircraft's capabilities and limitations better than we knew our own, which we had also thoroughly explored. There was no way we were going to endanger the aircraft or crew because our dad was watching. And while emergencies test your ability to think and react quickly and appropriately, we had all experienced enough at that point to not get rattled.

Surprisingly, however, Cdr. Remshak assigned Spike and me to fly the E-2 in the air demo for the tigers to be performed on May 30. It would be the same show we had done for the Pakistani dignitaries, sans bombs, live weapons fire, damaged radomes, and dead dolphins. It was unusual to let two JOs fly an airshow without adult supervision and Spike and I took advantage. We were supposed to fly by the ship at 200 feet of altitude, as Rich Payne had done with me in the right seat off the coast of Pakistan.

Instead, as CAG Orr berated us after I bagged an OK three wire: "You two sons-of-bitches—all we could see of your plane was the dome, until you pulled up in front of the bow like a bat out of hell." But he could not help smiling a bit as he said it. All in all, it was a memorable three days and a wake up.

The air wing flew off the next day. Spike, Otis, and I stayed aboard with our dads and sailed back into Coronado on June 1,

1989. The experience of thousands of husbands, fathers, sons, and brothers returning home after six months at sea was every bit as moving as manning the rails sailing into Pearl Harbor or watching flag draped caskets slide out the hanger doors to splash into the ocean. Husbands and wives embraced with joyous, tear-smeared faces. Children who hardly recognized their fathers, but whose mothers had read them their letters, leapt into their welcoming arms.

As I took in the chaotic, heartwarming scene, I felt proud that I swore to defend these people from an enemy in the USSR whose leader in 1956, Nikita Khrushchev, announced "we will bury you." And that our defensive effort, through an overwhelming but restrained offense, was succeeding. In fact, in December of 1991, the Soviet Union dissolved when Mikhail Gorbachev resigned as the first and last president of the USSR on Christmas Day (Khrushchev and his predecessors were titled *premier of the Soviet Union*) and turned over his presidential powers—including control of the nuclear launch codes—to Boris Yeltsin, the first president of the Russian Federation.

In 1989, at the peak of the Cold War, the US Navy had 792 ships. In 2020, at well under 300, we had fewer warships than at any time since 1916, and the number continues to dwindle. On the other hand, China, which has replaced the USSR as the world's greatest threat to democracy, increased its naval fleet to 355 ships by 2020, a 55 percent increase in less than fifteen years.

CHAPTER 12

RIGHT BACK TO WORK UPS

MOM, AUNT EDIE, AND SARAH flew down to San Diego to meet me and Dad. We enjoyed a fun couple of days eating out and catching up on all that I had missed at home since Thanksgiving. I took leave for the first two weeks in June and went back to Michigan to see the rest of my family and other friends there. I also needed to get down to Atlanta to visit my friend Charles Bowen, head to South Carolina for a wedding, and then pick up a girl I knew from college and had dated sporadically who agreed to drive out to California with me. Dad let me take his emerald green, 1967 Ford Fairlane convertible. The wedding and visiting Charles were both great fun. But my gal and I did not even make it out of South Carolina before we got into an argument about our future. She asked me to take her home. After dropping her off, I began a lonely, contemplative drive across the country to San Diego.

In February of 1990, the ship's crew was to sail *Connie* around South America to the Philadelphia Naval Shipyard where it underwent an $800-million, three-year Service Life Extension Program (SLEP). The Navy reassigned the Black Eagles and the rest of CVW-14 to the USS *Independence*, CV-62. The Navy commissioned the *Indy* in 1959, two years before *Connie*. It was the last of the Forrestal-class of aircraft carriers built by the United States. The *Connie*, CV-64, was the second of three Kitty Hawk-class carriers. Though a bit long in the tooth, the *Indy* was still a great ship. She served our country for thirty-nine years before the Navy decommissioned her in 1998.

The problem with changing ships was that the *Indy* was scheduled to deploy in June 1990. That left only a year after we got home from our first deployment before we would embark on our second. The normal turn-around time between cruises in those days was eighteen to twenty-four months. The short turn-around meant that junior pilots like Otis, Sausage, Snooze, and me, and Cdr. Gregor, who took over for Cdr. Remshak as CO, were in for a two-fer. If you were lucky, you could get through a three-year fleet assignment with only one six-month cruise. Spike and Junior were lucky. The others and I were not.

We kept busy for the next year. Cdr. Walt Joller became our XO, and we welcomed Lt. Cdr. Mike Wertz ("Turbo") and Lt.(jg)s Joe Petersen ("Chomp"), Marty Harrington ("Harv"), and Zeke Mowad (who needs a call sign when your name is Zeke?) as new pilots to the squadron, along with several new NFOs. We did not fly much over the summer while the planes went through post-cruise maintenance, just enough to maintain currency.

XO Joller and Turbo Wertz were great friends and accomplished runners. They both signed up to run the San Diego marathon that summer. Knowing that the race would be televised, they hatched a plot. When the starting gun fired, they both sprinted to the front of the pack and managed to hold the lead for the first mile. That initial burst of exertion hurt their finishing times, but they led the race—and caused the TV commentators some consternation about what to say about it—for the first four-and-a-half minutes.

College friends Kurt and Grace Kuelz, whose wedding I had attended in South Carolina, moved into the Poway house with me that summer, after I replaced the carpeting. I had to curtail my habit of going straight to the fenced in backyard pool after work, stripping off my flight suit, T-shirt, boots, and socks, and diving in to rinse away the day's worries. Otherwise, I genuinely enjoyed their company and we got along well. After a few months of sharing the house, however, they moved into their own apartment. Following their departure, while busy at work, I had little else to occupy my time. At night, I would lie awake on my bed in the otherwise empty house, overwhelmed by a bone-crushing loneliness.

After a slow summer, things ramped up. The Black Eagles spent September 6–October 15 on the *Connie* doing work ups. We then detached to El Centro from November 8–15, and then to Fallon, Nevada from November 26–December 15 to work with the fighters on air-to-air combat. We spent ten days at the end of January, February 27–March 22, and April 16–May 11 aboard the *Indy*, as well as four days in June aboard the USS *Nimitz*, CVN-68.

Our work up schedule caused me to miss Charles' wedding in Atlanta that fall. I did escape long enough to make it back to Michigan for high-school friend Brian Lazarus' marriage to our friend Paul's younger sister, Pam, and squadron mate Scott Harders' marriage to Mimi. Reif, Scott, two of Scott's non-Navy friends, and I flew back with him a week early. We sat in the back of the plane and flirted with the flight attendants while drinking the beverage cart dry. Mimi lived in Gross Point, next door to Grammy-winning singer and songwriter Anita Baker. We got to hear her mellifluous voice at about one o'clock one morning when she serenaded over the fence to us as we caroused in the hot tub: "You boys better tone it down, or I'm calling the cops."

I also attended a wedding and reception in Los Angeles, where my second cousin married the charming Patricia Mersch.

I managed to get arrested and charged with driving under the influence when Brian came out to visit in January. I was not even driving. While enjoying beers at Diego's in San Diego, we got into an argument about the lyrics to a song. We went out to my inconspicuous 1967 convertible to play the cassette (it was

1990) and settle our dispute. We took our beers with us. The police officer that arrested me wrote in his report that I started the car, but I only turned the key enough to turn on the radio. Regardless, Brian picked me up from the San Diego jail the next morning after they released me on my own recognizance. I pled the charges down to making an improper/unsafe lane change and paid a $530 fine. A bit ironic when I had not been driving, let alone changing lanes. Cdr. Gregor was not pleased.

I got arrested and again charged with DUI on the way home from the base after a Wednesday night happy hour a month before cruise. That one was legitimate and Skipper Gregor was downright angry about it, but he needed me and even liked me a little. I did not always make the best decisions in my personal life, but I was a good officer and a better pilot.

Following the release of *Top Gun* in 1986, the NAS Miramar Officers' Club took on a bit of a West Coast Studio 54 aura—without the drugs. As Maverick says to Goose in the movie, "This is what I call a target-rich environment." The closed-circuit televisions in the bar played videos of airplanes landing on and often crashing onto carrier decks. The club stocked sufficient footage of aircraft bursting into flames, ripping off landing gear, or smashing into planes parked alongside the landing area to keep the tape from being repetitive. The import may not have been subtle, but it could be effective.

Celebrities that were fans of the movie or naval aviation would come by the officers' club to hang out. Sidling up to a urinal one evening, I looked to my left to see Steven Stills of Crosby, Stills & Nash standing next to me. I told him I was a fan of his music. I did not try to shake his hand.

Jimmy Buffet is an accomplished pilot and went for a spin in the back of a Tomcat one sunny afternoon in Fightertown USA. He exited the jet ashen, apologizing to the crew that had to clean his lunch off the inside of the canopy. He made up for it by performing a couple of impromptu sets with a few Coral Reefers beside the officers club's outdoor pool. Ya gotta love swinging by the club for a beer after work and ending up at a private Jimmy Buffet concert.

In addition to my other duties that spring, I kept occupied at work by participating in one of the first classes of the Carrier Airborne Early Warning Weapons School, the much lamer E-2 version of Top Gun, in April. The E-2 was a critical air wing asset, yet it had no weapons or even countermeasures like flares or chaff. If the radar and NFO crew did their jobs flawlessly, the Tomcats or Hornets could take out any enemy aircraft seeking to shoot down the air wing's quarterback. But the Navy decided to teach E-2 pilots evasive tactics in the event a bandit (enemy aircraft) slipped through.

Because, as we often bragged to the gals at the officers' club, "the E-2 may be ugly, but it's slow," the defensive tactics we learned largely involved running away from a supersonic fighter at 350 knots. But all the E-2 pilots enjoyed pulling power, pressing the nose into a dive, racing toward the deck, and then practicing evading a missile or a fighter's bullets by rolling into and out of tight turns at full power and a few hundred feet of altitude.

Six months prior to deployment, the *Indy* hosted the Paramount production crew shooting the movie *Flight of the Intruder*. Paramount returned the favor by keeping the *Indy's* fire suppression team busy putting out small electrical fires started by their lighting equipment.

I attended Flight Deck Fire Fighting School for two days in June shortly before deployment. Students donned flame retardant suits and hoods before entering an aircraft hangar. Once inside, a large, perforated pipe at the rear of the hanger spewed flaming jet fuel toward the ceiling. Students wrangled large, wriggling, fire hoses, trying to direct the stream at the base of the fire. After practicing with the hoses, the instructors showed film from the fire aboard the USS *Ranger* in 1983 that killed six sailors and injured thirty-five others. We discussed lessons learned in a classroom. Being aboard a burning vessel loaded with fuel and ordinance in the middle of the ocean seemed like a worse idea than flying through a thunderstorm.

CHAPTER 13

WESTPAC JUNE TO DECEMBER 1990: OPERATION DESERT SHIELD

I DROVE THE FAIRLANE TO long term parking on Coronado Island shortly before midnight curfew on June 19, 1990. Eyeing *Indy's* dark mass in the distance, I put up the top, disconnected the battery, and lugged my bags over to her long aluminum gangplank. Lighted railings led me aboard. The Navy promoted me to the rank of lieutenant the year before, so instead of a six-pack, I would be sharing a two-man stateroom with Scott Harders. It was small, but with only two bunks suspended below the deck above, two desks underneath, and two narrow closets, we had plenty of room.

On the way to Hawaii, we conducted battle group exercises to get ready for another stint in the Indian Ocean. The Black Eagles kept a Hawkeye airborne around the clock for sixty hours, flying twenty flights in three days. We only had ten pilots on the *Indy* deployment, (on *Connie* we had eleven), so we all spent considerable time in the air. I set a personal record by logging a 4.9-hour flight, all at night, with Sausage on July 2.

We spent the Fourth of July in Waikiki before sailing farther west toward the Philippines. After departing Hawaii, flight time dried up. The air wing only flew about eight hours a day, four or five days a week. That only gave pilots three to four sorties a week—barely enough to keep current.

When we crossed the international date line and skipped from July 8 to July 10, the *Indy's* skipper, Captain Thomas S. Slater, shared his sense of humor with the crew.

USS INDEPENDENCE
CV-62

12 July 1990

We crossed the international date line the other day which meant we went from July 8 to July 10 overnight. The ship graciously declared July 9 to be Junior Officer Appreciation Day. It is nice losing a day of cruise like that, however on the way back it means we have the same day twice in a row. Pretty weird.

Because of local unrest in the Philippine Islands, the admiral restricted liberty to the base at Subic Bay and seven blocks surrounding it in Olongapo. Being PI veterans, that did not deter us much. You could get a Jeepney driver who knew how to avoid the check points to take you to the Barrio or Subic City for a couple of *multi-colored beer tickets*, as we called foreign currency. Jeepneys were small, crowded busses found throughout Philippine cities and barrios.

The night of July 25, after departing the PI, we lost an A-6 Intruder and crew on a bombing exercise. The Intruder's wingman saw the jet explode as it impacted the water. There was no need to conduct search and rescue for the pilot and bombardier/navigator and the air wing flew the planned flight schedule the next day. With witnesses to this tragedy, as opposed to the EA-6B that simply never returned on my first cruise, and continued flight operations, we seemed to move past this loss more quickly. The somber service, where I witnessed a second burial at sea, also helped, as did the levity of the Crossing the Line Ceremony on July 31, where as a Shellback I devilishly administered the initiation rites I had endured a year before.

Carrier Group One took over Indian Ocean duty and planned to stay there through August, September, and early October. After that, we planned to visit Australia again, this time Sydney, and a few other ports while steaming home, arriving shortly before Christmas. Saddam Hussein, the "Butcher of Baghdad," changed our plans when he ordered four Iraqi Revolutionary Guard heavy divisions, and the equivalent of a fifth composed of special operations commandos, to invade neighboring Kuwait on August 2, 1990. US military aid during Iraq's 1980–1988 war with Iran had made it the fourth-largest army in the world at that time. Five days after the invasion, President George H.W. Bush ordered the organization of Operation Desert Shield.

We were due to dock at Diego Garcia for a two-day respite on the third of August. Instead, we hastily steamed northwest, arriving on station in the Gulf of Oman on the fifth.

USS INDEPENDENCE
CV-62

8 August 1990

Hello from the Persian Gulf. By the time you get this I am sure you will know more about what is going on from CNN than I do from all the secret messages I read. Suffice it to say that I am fine and there is no need to worry. We lost our port visit in Diego Garcia when we were ordered up to the Gulf. No big deal though, it was only two days and this is kinda exciting.

The battle group patrolled the Gulf alone for the rest of August and most of September under the command of Rear Admiral Jerry L. Unruh. To the west, the USS *Dwight D. Eisenhower*, CVN-69, sailed from the Mediterranean into the Red Sea. During that time, President Bush collaborated with allies in Australia, Europe, Japan, and the Middle East to develop a coalition to respond to Iraqi's unacceptable attack on a sovereign neighbor. Iraq's only access to the sea was at the port of Basra, sandwiched between Iraq's rival to the east since antiquity, Iran, and tiny Kuwait to the south. President Hussein invaded Kuwait to take over its more advanced refinery facilities and ports at the north end of the Persian Gulf, thinking the world would not notice or care enough to respond. He was mistaken. The free world, led by the United States, proved unprepared to let a murderous, fanatical, leader like Saddam Hussein take over an oil-rich, strategically located neighbor. Moreover, the unprovoked attack on Kuwait posed a threat to Saudi Arabia. If Hussein were to take over that country as well, it would control twenty percent of the world's oil supply.

The air wing spent a week flying only at night, creating havoc with our sleep cycles. After that, we settled into a more reasonable operating schedule of flying from noon to midnight, five or six days a week, devoting the other day or two to maintenance on the aircraft and flight deck. One endless duty aboard a carrier is the *FOD walkdown*. FOD (foreign object debris) can be any object that doesn't belong on a flight deck: a screw, knob, pen, chess piece, or other debris. If a turbine engine sucks up FOD, bad things happen. To avoid this, before flight ops, often several times a day, rain or shine, the crew forms lines and walks the flight deck shoulder to shoulder from bow to stern, scouring for FOD. Enlisted personnel were required to participate when on duty and not otherwise occupied. Officers had discretion, but the enlisted noticed who participated and who did not.

It was hot in the Gulf of Oman in August and September, a hundred degrees or more on the flight deck. After conducting the aircraft preflight checks in a Nomex flight suit, flight harness, and helmet (with foam noise suppressors inserted in your ear canals to keep the screeching jet engines at bay) and firing up the engines, the catapult usually shot you off the carrier soaked in sweat. Sometimes, when launching after dark with a slight breeze, you were merely uncomfortably damp.

After forty-five days at sea, we earned a beer day, a "celebration" we had gladly avoided on my first cruise. Navies throughout history have recognized that weeks at sea are a trying experience. The United States Navy adopted a policy that if a warship spent forty-five consecutive days at sea, without allowing the crew to get off and walk on solid ground, they got a beer day. The *Indy*'s skipper, Capt. Richard L. Ellis, Jr., who replaced Capt. Slater in July, ordered the COD to fly 10,000 beers out to the carrier, two per man, and held a steel beach picnic with alcohol. As a Scotch-Irish Catholic, I bartered with the Muslims and Mormons for their beer chits and turned it into a real party.

The battle group formed a quarantine on the Persian Gulf at the Strait of Hormuz, between the northern tip of the United Arab Emirates (UAE) and the southern coast of Iran. The idea was to restrict Iraq from shipping oil, its primary source of revenue. But as weeks turned into months, we took no decisive action. Further, the Bush administration ordered us to allow any ship with an alleged humanitarian purpose to transit into or out of the Gulf. The quarantine became porous. Iraq, of course, exploited our lenience. We wondered why we were twiddling our thumbs on an aircraft carrier with seventy aircraft ready, willing, and able to make things right.

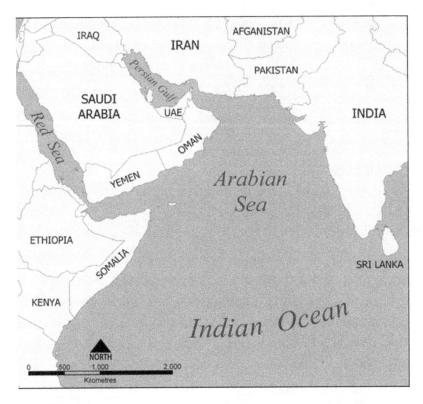

As the weeks dragged on, we did what we could to attempt to break up the monotony.

USS INDEPENDENCE
CV-62

15 August 1990

We had a chess tournament on the ship. It is still going on but I lost in the third round yesterday to one of our mess cooks. He was good. Andy Dressel and I entered from our squadron and we both lost in the third round. It was a nice diversion.

On September 19, after nearly two months at sea, the *Indy* dropped anchor and the crew stood down for twelve hours, except for alerts. My department head, Mark Copenberger, flew into Riyad, Saudi Arabia for two weeks to liaison with the command center, so I organized and ran a safety stand down for the Black Eagles.

USS INDEPENDENCE
CV-62

24 September 1990

The stand down went well. It was short, which made everyone happy. We also had some fun that day when all the air wing officers got out brooms and fire hoses and scrubbed down the flight deck. It has gotten pretty slippery with all the oil, fuel, and hydraulic fluid that gets spilled on it and the non-skid is wearing away. Of course, there were water fights with the fire hoses and some other general screwing around, which gave us a chance to blow off some steam. We got some sun and managed to get the flight deck fairly clean too.

After lamenting that the admiral had cancelled all liberty, including my planned trip to Bahrain with Maintenance Control Officer Troy Vanwormer, I noted:

The good news is that we've been approved to receive imminent danger pay ($110/month) oh boy. That's $208 flight pay, $110 flight deck pay, and $110 imminent danger. If what I was doing wasn't dangerous, I'd be broke.

Realizing how worrisome this might sound to my mom and dad, I closed with:

> Not to worry though, we're well away from Iraq and the entire Air Force and Marine Corps are between us and them.

That changed in early October, when Admiral Unruh ordered the *Indy* to sail through the Strait of Hormuz. It would be the first carrier to enter the shallow, confined Persian Gulf since 1974. I was not aboard.

At 0430 on October 2, 1990, Chomp and I, along with a top NFO crew, launched off the catapult into the still, predawn sky. Our mission: provide cover—along with a dozen fighters and bombers and a handful of S-3s—as the *Indy* traversed into the Persian Gulf. We were all in range of Iranian missiles as we guarded the carrier.

CIC radioed: "Any enemy aircraft?"

"Negative," we replied.

"Missile locks?"

"Not yet."

Once the ship passed safely through the Strait of Hormuz without any Iraqi or Iranian resistance, we banked our planes south toward Masirah Island off the coast of Oman at the northwestern edge of the Arabian Sea. Landing in Masirah, we witnessed a massive military build-up. Thousands of boots were on the ground, including allies from Great Britain and France, under the Omani's cautiously watchful eye.

It is indeed a small world. While wandering amongst the thousands of marines, soldiers, and sailors, I ran into Mike Renie, a fraternity brother from Georgia Tech who was flying P-3s out of Masirah on a detachment. I grabbed a nap on a cot in his air conditioned four-man room and then flew my second 4.9-hour mission of the cruise, landing back at Masirah at 0200. Mike and I caught up for a couple of hours after that before I grabbed another nap and flew a third mission.

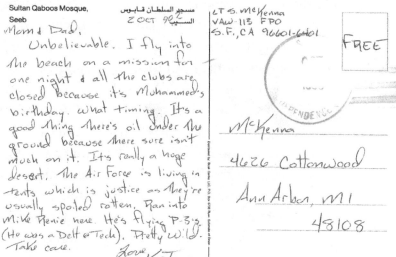

Postcard home from Masirah

We recovered back aboard the *Indy* on October 3. The five of us in the crew spent thirty-four hours off the ship, fourteen of them in the air, but it was a nice break. And I got to bag a day trap on an aircraft carrier doing what the United States designed and built it to do—in the Persian Gulf.

Having sailed right up to the Iraqi's and Iranian's doorstep, with the UAE, Saudi Arabia, and Yemen looking on, knocked, waited for a response, and received none beyond political caterwauling, we sailed back out of the Gulf a few days later. It was uncomfortable to be in a narrow gulf with Iran to the north and, at best, fair-weather friends to the south, despite the carrier's formidable firepower and defenses.

After two months on station, the admiral reinstated liberty and the ship implemented trips ashore for officers who were going stir crazy. Scott took five days of leave in Bahrain. I enjoyed having my own room but would have rather visited Bahrain. Otis spent two weeks in Riyadh, Saudi Arabia. I got to fly a lot, including a low-level over the desert of Oman.

Planning the flight gave me a greater appreciation for bomber pilots and navigators. I precisely calculated scores of checkpoints along the route, doing the math to time turns to the second while flying prescribed speeds, altitudes, and headings along a two-hour route through majestic ravines framed by the Al Hajar Mountains. Harv and I spent extra time during the preflight brief discussing how best to fly a large turboprop airplane on a low-level flight.

I only scared Harv—and myself—once. After pulling around a craggy, time-worn peak, I rolled out to see a wall of rock close ahead that had not been (or I had missed) on the topographical map. Adding full power, I pulled the yoke back hard and watched the g-meter hit its limit as we narrowly cleared its towering height. I have an entertaining video of the flight that Harv filmed on a video camera. After that flight in the morning, the skipper and Otis planned to fly the route in the afternoon. Cdr. Gregor went med-down, however, so I volunteered to ride in Otis' right seat. That was a fun day. As I wrote home on October 16: *I think I would prefer to fly around down on the deck with mountains above me on either side than up doing circles at 24,000 feet.*

The CODs and other supply aircraft prioritized shipments of troops and equipment into Masirah and Saudi Arabia, often leaving the mail behind. When you did hear from home you tried your best to keep up with things like college football, family, and friends. After nearly three months at sea, however, home seemed even further away than the 10,000 miles it was.

In addition to the low levels, Skipper Gregor authorized NFOs to ride in the cockpit during flights. We flew around enforcing a no-fly zone that Iraq and Iran dared not violate, while waiting for somebody to start shooting at us. Thus, the NFOs, who would normally be busy coordinating a strike or conducting air intercept patrol, did not have that much to do beyond monitoring radios. I spent a few flights in the tube listening to David Bowie on my Walkman and writing letters while Jeff Hudgens, Fred Shelton, or Rob Bowen got to experience a cat shot and trap from the cockpit and view Oman, its gulf, Yemen, Saudi Arabia, Iran, and Pakistan from 24,000 feet.

Bored, we invented *astronaut qualifications*.

To qualify as an E-2 "astronaut," you unstrapped from your harness, got up, and walked into the center of the aircraft, by the door. The pilot then pushed the nose over for seven seconds (the oil pumps would cavitate after eight) while you leaned forward and floated weightlessly. Those were not authorized, but they were not prohibited either. Nonetheless, we did not do them when the crew included the skipper, XO, or a department head.

On one flight with a JO crew, I decided to do an aileron roll. I had been thinking about it for a while. An aileron roll is when you raise the nose and then roll the aircraft 360 degrees around the aircraft's longitudinal axis running nose to tail. The E-2 was limited to a sixty-degree angle of bank, but an aileron roll is a one-g maneuver if you do it properly. You may have seen the video of air show pilot Bob Hoover executing the maneuver while pouring water from a pitcher into a glass without spilling a drop. If not, you should check it out. At that point, I had over 1,500 hours and nearly 200 traps in the E-2. I could say I was testing the aircraft in case a bandit jumped us, but I just knew I could roll the plane safely, I was bored, and it would be fun.

I turned to Otis in the right seat and raised a green, Nomex gloved finger to my lips. Pushing the throttles forward we accelerated from on station speed of 140 knots to 200. I pulled the nose up and rolled left, feeding in rudder to assist the roll and keep the nose straight. As we rolled inverted, I reversed the rudder input and the aircraft completed the maneuver as expected. Rob Bowen ("Sluggo," due to his buzz cut and resemblance to the character from the *Nancy* comic strip) was watching his radar scope as mission commander. He noticed the world spin and radioed up to the cockpit:

"What was that?"

"No idea what you're talking about," I replied.

We all grinned at each other during postflight and never said a word.

On October 21, after ninety days at sea, we got our second beer day. While welcome, the celebration was muted. The crew had assumed a grim, resolute countenance. Halloween marked day one hundred on station in the Arabian Sea and the Gulf of Oman atop the Indian Ocean. There was no trick-or-treating or partying, just a one-hundredth straight day of dangerous, demanding work on the other side of the world.

The *Indy's* crew and the air wing were both bored and anxious. We had been flying missions in hostile territory, Intruders laden with 500-pound bombs, Tomcats carrying Phoenix, Sidewinder, and Sparrow missiles, and Hornets hauling both bombs and missiles, for three months straight, without dropping or firing any. Meanwhile, Saddam Hussein's troops remained in Kuwait and started burning oil in the Gulf. This turned the already stiflingly hot air you breathed acrid with tarry smoke. This affront was mild, however, in comparison to the environmental devastation caused by a defeated, but spiteful Hussein, whose Revolutionary Guard torched 600 Kuwaiti oil wells the following year.

The USS *Midway*, CV-41, based in Yokosuka, Japan at the time, relieved us of responsibility for Gonzo Station on November 2, 1990. The Navy commissioned the *Midway* on September 10, 1945, eight days after Japan's surrender in World War II.

Capt. Ellis asked for port visits to Thailand and Hong Kong on the way home, along with the obligatory stop for maintenance and supplies in the PI. Port visits were never set in stone and we all wasted time fantasizing about where we might get to visit and what we would do there. Sydney was out of the question at that point, being thousands of miles away in a different hemisphere. The Navy said no to Thailand and Hong Kong as well. Instead, we spent November 11–14 in Singapore, followed by a week at Subic Bay. On my first WestPac, we visited Hawaii, the Philippines, Diego Garcia, Perth, Thailand, Hong Kong, Alaska, and Seattle before returning home. On my second, we made brief visits to Hawaii, the Philippines, and Singapore, and I got to fly into and spend a few hours on Masirah.

Skipper Gregor tapped me to fly the E-2 in the air wing airshow for dignitaries the day before we pulled into Singapore. Recalling my stunt with Spike on the previous Tiger Cruise, however, he pulled me aside and said: "Steve, I am giving you a direct order not to fly by the ship below 200 feet." Lt. Cdr. John "Loot" LaBella, a great pilot with top-notch stick and rudder skills, rode in the right seat. We had fun racing past the side of the carrier at 350 knots and then pulling up across the bow in front of a packed crowd on the flight deck, even at 200 feet.

I would describe our visit to Singapore as dystopian—the city was overly clean and orderly with police in starched white uniforms everywhere. I did not particularly enjoy the visit. The Singaporean police arrested Snooze for the crime of being *drunk and sleepy* when he fell asleep on a park bench after a night at the clubs, affirming his callsign.

A little over a week after departing Singapore, Chomp and I flew in early to Subic Bay on November 25, where the mechanics started getting the planes ready for post-cruise corrosion inspections. I have no recollection or written record of what we did for Thanksgiving that year.

December 9 happened twice when we crossed the international date line on the way east to Hawaii. We manned the rails again as we sailed into Pearl Harbor on the thirteenth for a CINCPAC (commander in charge Pacific) post-deployment meeting. CINCPAC, Admiral Charles Larson, came aboard the *Indy* beforehand to commend the crew on a job well done. As I wrote home: *This will delay liberty call about three hours. I wish they'd stop doing us favors.*

On the way back to San Diego, the air wing planned to fly off the carrier and back home to Miramar on December 18. The press, however, found Operation Desert Shield newsworthy. They wanted to cover the fly-off from the ship. But they could not get aboard until the nineteenth, delaying our fly-off, after six months of a grueling tour of duty, by a day. Fortunately, no intrepid reporter interviewed me to hear what I thought about that.

That afternoon, Otis and I tucked in under the skipper's starboard wing as dash-2 in the four-plane formation of E-2s flying into Miramar. Upon landing, we all celebrated another heartwarming homecoming. While delighted to be home, it weighed a bit that there was no one special to meet me.

The Black Eagle pilots won two of three Golden Tailhook competitions on that cruise, while also beating out the other seven fixed-wing squadrons for the highest overall landing grades and boarding rate.

CHAPTER 14

PAYING THE PIPER AND MOVING ON

I WAS UNABLE TO VISIT my family for Christmas that year. For one thing, Scott and I overslept in our hotel room in Hawaii, missed curfew, and nearly missed the ship's departure on the way home. As punishment, Skipper Gregor made the two of us alternate as squadron duty officer over the Christmas and New Year holidays. We joked that we felt like the wolf and the sheepdog punching the time clock in and out of work in that old *Looney Tunes* cartoon. The upside to our punishment: our squadronmates with wives and kids got to spend more time with them over the holidays. Scott's wife was busy with a medical residency, so he was almost as much a bachelor as I. The other reason: CINCPAC put the *Indy* on a thirty-day alert and the air wing on a ninety-six-hour tether—we could take leave, but only had ninety-six hours to report back to base to quickly work up and deploy again in case things blew up in the Persian Gulf.

Things did blow up in the Gulf on January 17, 1991, when the US-led allied coalition launched Operation Desert Storm. The media covered the "shock and awe" of the allied bombardment relentlessly. I learned of the attack while waving FCLPs alongside the runway in El Centro that evening. Sluggo, the squadron duty officer, passed the news along over the radio. "It's about time," I said to Zeke Mowad, while we graded the pilots doing touch-and-gos next to us.

The United States and forty allies, including Arab nations, flew more than 18,000 air deployment missions, more than 116,000 combat air sorties, and dropped 88,500 tons of bombs (500 tons more than the *Indy* weighed) in the largest air campaign since Vietnam. After six weeks of unimpeded air attacks, the ground campaign lasted only a hundred hours before the allies liberated Kuwait. US troops taking part in the war totaled 697,000, with 299 losing their lives. President George H.W. Bush decided to stop short of invading Baghdad—a measured, but controversial decision that I agreed with.

President Bush served as a naval aviator in WWII, after also completing his training at NAS Corpus Christi. After successfully bombing a Japanese installation on the island of Chichijima, his TBF Avenger was hit and went down. While two other crew members were killed, President Bush bailed out and was rescued. I had the privilege of meeting him years after the Gulf War when he spoke at a retreat for Gibson Dunn, the law firm I worked for at the time. He was charming and eloquent.

Thankfully, Admiral Larson did not order the *Indy* or CVW-14 back to the Gulf. As exciting as it would have been to participate in Operation Desert Storm, I was not anxious to move back aboard a carrier and sail halfway around the world again for a third cruise, having returned from my second less than a month before. Since joining the Black Eagles twenty-one months prior, I had spent twelve months on WestPac deployments, several more aboard ship or in Fallon, Nevada during work-ups and other exercises, and countless nights aboard various carriers during CQ.

One thing I did not look forward to upon returning to San Diego was addressing my second pre-deployment arrest. The San Diego District Attorney's Office had not forgotten about it. Nor did the assistant DA assigned to my case care that I was now a decorated combat pilot. I pled guilty in January and the court sentenced me to forty-eight hours of roadside work (orange vest and all), a $990 fine, completion of San Diego's First Offender Program, enrollment in the Navy's Alcohol and Drug Substance Abuse Program (NADSAP) for six months, six months of AA meetings, and five years of probation.

The NADSAP program entailed two weeks of full-time counseling and classes in a group setting. I do not enjoy talking about my feelings, especially amongst strangers, but did my best. Upon graduation in March, the Miramar Counseling and Assistance Center gave me the Level II Growth Award. I got my driver's license back in June after completing the three-month First Offender Program.

Cdr. Joller—a fantastic officer, leader, mentor, and friend who was senselessly struck and killed by a car while riding his bicycle home from base many years later—succeeded Cdr. Gregor as the Black Eagle's CO. He ranked me as his top lieutenant on my last fitness report, giving me a wide choice of options for my next tour of duty. I debated between going back to Pensacola to teach students to fly the T-2 or seeking a job as an instructor pilot in the RAG. When Cdr. Remshak sought me out and asked me to be a RAG instructor I agreed on the spot, thrilled both with the job and the idea of serving under Skipper Remshak again. I flew my last four flights as a Black Eagle with Chomp, Otis, Turbo, and Harv on April 30 and May 2, 1991—fantastic company to fly with in my last days in the fleet.

CHAPTER 15

A FIREBIRD ONCE AGAIN

I STARTED MY NEW JOB as an instructor pilot and LSO in the RAG at the end of May 1991. VAW-110 Firebird instructors like Andy Jones, Jay Adelman, and Pete Tomczak got me and my contemporaries, Joe Mock, Dave Busse, Marnel Alexis, and others up to speed on the differences between learning and teaching the difficult E-2C RAG syllabus. By August, we started instructing students. I thoroughly enjoyed teaching young pilots to fly the quirky E-2C Hawkeye. Sitting in the right seat during their first landings, especially on the carrier—restraining hands that desperately wanted to take the controls—was both terrifying and terribly rewarding.

I met my future wife, again, in early summer. I got a call one evening from Patricia Mersch, the beautiful bride from the Los Angeles wedding I had attended two years prior. She was shooting video footage for Nissan Motor Corporation in LA and asked if I would like to meet. Patricia became close with my parents after marrying my cousin and moving to Michigan. The marriage was rocky, and my mom and dad provided consolation through her divorce. They suggested she look me up while on the West Coast. Mom and Dad hoped Patricia would set me up with one of her cultured friends in Santa Monica; perhaps the lovely Kate McMurray, Fred MacMurray and June Haver's daughter, who had been maid of honor at Patricia's first wedding. It did not quite work out that way.

I drove the Fairlane to Del Mar to meet Patricia at Jake's by the Sea for dinner. She blew me away. More gorgeous than I remembered, with shining, ebony hair framing dazzling hazel eyes and an enchanting smile. And so interesting and easy to talk to—beauty and brains. We shared our thoughts for hours in the restaurant, and a couple more in her rented Cadillac after the staff at Jake's asked us to leave so they could close. Upon parting, I drove back to San Diego and lay awake half the night thinking of her. At one point, I got out of bed and left a recording on her answering machine of Rod Stewart's "Heart and Soul." She had captured mine.

At work, eager to swap stories from the first combat missions flown since the Vietnam War, my fellow instructors and I looked forward to the annual Tailhook convention that September. A couple thousand carrier aviators gathering in Las Vegas after an overwhelming victory in the Persian Gulf, what could go wrong?

In hindsight, Skipper Remshak might have thought better about allowing the squadron to host a leg shaving station—where young ladies gladly volunteered to have their legs shaved by lascivious aviators—even with a strict no touching above mid-thigh order. That did not play well in the ensuing investigation. Neither did my conduct, which was certainly unbecoming of an officer. I had just completed my mandated six-month abstinence from alcohol prior to Tailhook and was imbibing vigorously. While quaffing beers at a crowded outdoor pool, some friends and I spied a shapely young woman with beautiful long, dark hair that fell below her bikini bottoms. A fellow instructor made a crude sexual innuendo and dared me to go touch her hair with my penis. I did, like an idiot and a pervert. The girl turned around as I quickly slunk away. Embarrassed and remorseful, I stumbled back to my room, called Patricia to profess my love, and fell asleep. The more serious sexual assaults were alleged to have taken place that night, while I snored in my bed. Those allegations led to a massive investigation that seemed to take on a life of its own and would come back to haunt me.

In October, Patricia and I rented a large, white house on a hill overlooking San Clemente. I proposed the day before Thanksgiving while strolling along the beach below the San Clemente Pier. I saved the strip of paper from a fortune cookie that read "Accept the next proposal you hear" and wrapped it around the ring. Dropping to one knee, I pretended to find the engagement ring in the sand. Looking up at Patricia I took her hand, put the ring in it, and proposed, asking her to marry and spend the rest of her life with me. She accepted!

I called her father, John, beforehand and received his blessing. He and Patricia's mother Virginia ("Gigi"), brother Jay, his wife Anne, and their three young children joined us for Thanksgiving the next day. John gave a wonderful toast to our upcoming life together before we dug into the turkey, stuffing, and mashed potatoes.

John's family had run a large, successful textile factory in Luxembourg. John's older brother Charlot signed a contract to supply the Nazis at the start of World War II, prompting John to leave the hometown that bore his surname and become a diplomat for the Allies. Hitler's forces interred and tortured John for three years before he escaped.

Gigi hailed from Massachusetts and studied in Switzerland before graduating from Wellesley College in 1940. She served with the Office of War Information in London during the war. She lived through the nightly bombings the Luftwaffe inflicted on the United Kingdom's capital city. Once, she shared an elevator with Winston Churchill and his family. Would that the so-called leaders of today mingled with the people instead of sequestering themselves in ivory towers, insisting on private security to protect them from those they swore to serve.

John and Gigi met and fell in love on the French Riviera after the Allies took Berlin. They married in London in April of 1946 and lived in Luxembourg for four years before moving to the United States. After touring our beautiful country, they settled in Los Angeles, California.

Patricia and I got married on July 11, 1992, in Michigan. I highly recommend an easily memorable anniversary date like 7-11. The wedding service took place on a hot and humid Saturday evening in Ann Arbor. One of my groomsmen and one of Patricia's bridesmaids nearly fainted during the ceremony. Dad and Uncle Pat helped them down the aisle after Patricia and I each said, "I do."

Spike flew in for the rehearsal dinner and wedding from Patuxent River, Maryland, where, on CAG Orr's strong recommendation, he pulled off getting orders to attend and then instruct at the Navy's Test Pilot School. Reif, then flying for American Airlines, made it as well. Fellow Firebirds Otis, Junior, Harv, Gary Gates, and Joe Kerstiens scheduled cross-country flights to Michigan and flew out in two E-2s.

Following the wedding, six shipmates assembled on the stone walkway in front of the church. Otis gave the commands:

"Forward, march." Officers in pressed navy-blue trousers and white jackets adorned with shoulder boards, wings, and medals marched in unison up the walkway, swords held vertically in white-gloved hands at their sides.

"Ready, halt." The officers clicked polished heels together and stood at attention.

"Center, face." Each executed a left or right face to stand across from their counterpart.

"Present, swords." Arms extended swords skyward at forty-five-degree angles, forming an arch of swords anchored by my friends and fellow aviators.

Patricia took my arm as we walked through the arch while the guests looked on. Exiting, Otis slapped Patricia on her backside with the flat of his sword and declared:

"Welcome to the Navy!"

Patricia jumped, gasped, and then turned to me and smiled.

Travis Point Country Club, where my parents moved after I went to Georgia Tech, hosted the reception. After I left home, my parents tired of the one-hundred-year-old farmhouses on acres of land I had grown up in, upgrading to a beautiful new condominium on a golf course. *What the hell!* But the club hosted a jubilant reception, complete with chicken, salmon, or steak, and of course a stage and live band.

The previous February, after six months as a RAG instructor, Cdr. Remshak designated me the COMNAVAIRPAC (Commander Naval Air Pacific) E-2C pilot NATOPS evaluator. My studious nature and engineering background provided me with sound knowledge of how the various systems of the E-2C operated and interacted. As the evaluator for all six E-2C fleet squadrons in the Pacific theatre, along with the reserve squadrons and the RAG, I evaluated the evaluators.

The NATOPS officer in each squadron, and instructors in the RAG, gave annual proficiency checks to all E-2 pilots. I made sure they administered the checks uniformly and covered all aspects of operating the aircraft safely, from preflight briefing to postflight documentation. It took a couple of days to go through the training records and other paperwork maintained by the Safety Department to ensure it was all current and correct. After that, the squadron NATOPS officer flew a check flight from the right seat while I questioned him about systems and simulated emergencies in the aircraft to evaluate his reactions. It was a demanding, fulfilling job, with responsibility for the safe, standardized operation of forty $90 million aircraft.

The Pentagon decided to update the E-2C around that time, with upgraded engines and radar, among other things. As the COMNAVAIRPAC NATOPS evaluator, I also assumed the role of E-2C Plus model manager. The upgrades required significant revisions to the NATOPS manual and procedures. I spent countless hours poring over the manual and noting where it needed changes. Toward the end of my time in the Navy, when the Operational Action Group Executive Steering Committee met in Norfolk in the fall of 1993 to address the rewrite, I helped plan the meetings and represented VAW-110 and the E-2 fleet squadrons on the West Coast and in Japan. It was a productive week. Representatives from the Pentagon, Grumman, and the navies of allies Singapore and Japan discussed and drafted revised procedures for operating the upgraded aircraft.

Not too long after assuming my role as NATOPS evaluator, I faced a challenge. I walked down the hall to a fleet squadron's ready room to give their NATOPS officer his check flight. I had reviewed the squadron's paperwork the week before and found several discrepancies. Part of the NATOPS check was a written test. The squadron NATOPS officer passed, but barely.

The check flight started out poorly during the brief. The pilot failed to calculate our *go speed*. This is a simple calculation you made from the tables in the back of the NATOPS manual to determine—based on weight, pressure altitude, temperature, wind, and runway length—the speed at which you commit to going airborne. If you lose an engine, blow a tire, sprout a leak, or catch fire after go speed, you continue the takeoff and deal with it airborne. If you try to abort the takeoff above go speed, you are liable to run off the runway. His reasoning for not making this important calculation:

"We've got more than enough runway to get airborne."

"True enough," I agreed, "but that's not the only reason to calculate go speed, is it?"

He did not perform much better on preflight when he was unable to identify a couple of the more obscure pieces of onboard equipment. The flight itself was okay, safe but unimpressive.

During the debrief, I outlined my concerns and told the pilot I needed to talk to my skipper. Cdr. William J. Tyson III, an East Coast pilot extraordinaire rumored to have done an aileron roll in an E-2 as a junior officer, took over for Cdr. Remshak as skipper of the RAG in August of 1992. I knocked on his door and asked if I could have a word. After closing the door behind me, I went through the various discrepancies noted during my inspection and check flight. While the pilot was competent, I felt that his complacency was dangerous. In my view, he had failed the NATOPS check. While pilots occasionally did not pass a NATOPS check, it was rare. For the squadron NATOPS officer to fail one just did not happen. The squadron would have to revamp its entire NATOPS program, something we had voluntarily implemented while I was the Black Eagles' NATOPS officer.

Skipper Tyson asked me a few questions and after a discussion concurred with my assessment. He walked down the hall with me to break the news to the squadron CO. That move garnered a bit of resentment; who was I to down an entire squadron? But I also earned some respect for doing the right thing instead of the easy thing. During the remainder of my time as the NATOPS evaluator, before ceding responsibility to Joe Mock, a great pilot and friend, the squadrons' paperwork was properly completed and the pilots were prepared.

I also created a stir when I gave a down to a female student who performed poorly on a RAG syllabus flight. Instructors frequently downed students in early flight training. By the time they got to the RAG, however, students were expected to, and ordinarily did, perform syllabus maneuvers at least proficiently, if not perfectly, on their first attempt. A few senior officers grilled me on my decision to award the down, which required two remedial flights before trying again. This would not have occurred with a male student. I stood my ground and truthfully stated that I harbored no bias against the pilot based on her gender.

"Look," I explained, "she simply did not perform the required maneuvers at a satisfactory level. She needs a couple extra flights to get them right before continuing with the syllabus." Cdr. Tomasoski had replaced Cdr. Tyson as the RAG CO by that time and backed my decision. We even talked to the CO of NAS Miramar, Capt. Skip Braden, a strong leader who concurred that we should not treat a female student any differently than a male. Having been named Instructor of the Quarter the previous year, flown with "Ski" as a Black Eagle, and recently given Capt. Braden his annual NATOPS check, I had credibility. I graded hard, but fairly.

Considering political correctness when training a person—male or female—to safely operate an aircraft with four other people on board whose lives depend on the pilot's competency disturbed me. I believed then as I do now that a persons' genitalia or skin color should never be considered—either positively or negatively—when evaluating people. Once you let immutable physical characteristics like gender or race into the equation, you are no longer evaluating fairly. In general, men are physically stronger and faster than women, but that does not negate the fact that some women are more physically gifted than most men (even putting childbirth aside). I certainly would not want to fight Rhonda Rousey, play tennis against Serena Williams, or challenge Katie Ledecky to a swim race.

In January of 1993, the VAW-115 Liberty Bells in Atsugi, Japan, were due for their annual NATOPS check. I flew commercial to Japan, in coach while the airlines still allowed smoking on the fifteen-hour flight. I spent the first couple of days recovering from jet lag while getting to know the pilots and NFOs in the squadron and going over training records, which were in good order. I then conducted check flights for VAW-115's NATOPs officer, commanding officer, and another pilot. On each, we plotted routes that took us to and around Mt. Fuji, the spectacular volcanic peak that rises, often through billowing clouds, to 12,388 feet. It towers over the island of Honshū in central Japan like a snow-capped beacon. The Liberty Bells taught me some Japanese, long since forgotten, and showed me a grand time, including a trip into the bustling city of Tokyo upon completing the NATOPS checks.

In June of 1993, I flew back to NAS Norfolk to face my fate for my part in the 1991 Tailhook scandal, as it came to be called. Early in the investigation, the fellow instructor who had made the dare, along with a former shipmate with whom I confided, turned me in. I did not deny the incident. I do my best not to lie, especially when it is important.

Skipper Tyson flew back with me for Admiral's Mast. I stood before Vice Admiral J.P. Reason, the commander in charge, Naval Surface Forces, US Atlantic Fleet. After I sincerely apologized, Cdr. Tyson vouched for me being an exemplary officer, aviator, and instructor, despite my colossal lapse of judgment in Las Vegas.

Over forty Navy and Marine officers received punishment. Admiral Reason, who became the Navy's first African American four-star admiral in 1996, gave me a nonjudicial letter of admonition for conduct unbecoming an officer (indecent exposure) and a $1,000 fine. Having submitted my letter of resignation in October of 1992, shortly after marrying Patricia, I will never know if the letter would have been a career ender. What it did do was make me realize I needed to curtail my drinking. Patricia moving in with me a month after Tailhook was a godsend and I have not had any further incidents with alcohol and the law in over thirty years.

The Tailhook scandal, in part, led Secretary of Defense Les Aspin to announce a new policy on the assignment of women to the armed forces in April 1993. He ordered the services to allow women to compete for assignments in combat aircraft. He also ordered the Navy to open additional ships to women and draft a proposal for Congress to remove existing legislative barriers to assigning women to combat vessels. I was honored to instruct some of the first females to learn to fly the E-2.

Reflecting on all the above, I composed this essay in applying for law school:

The Changing Face of the Navy

"It is killing . . . and it is . . . uncivilized! And women cannot do it! ... I think the very nature of women disqualifies them . . . Women give life. Sustain life. Nurture life. They do not take it."
General Robert H. Barrow
USMC, retired

Since the beginnings of recorded history men have been fighting wars. The United States Navy is no exception. During my three-and-a-half years of operational sea duty as a navy pilot, the wardrooms and warships of the military were the exclusive environs of men. Recently however, with a more liberal White House and a recent Tailhook scandal, women are infiltrating these bastions of manhood. In 1973, when women first began flying naval aircraft, their only assignments were to nontactical planes. Today, we are beginning to see women with orders to combat squadrons. Even more unsettling to some is that these women will be serving with their squadrons on combat ships.

Fact: many Navy men do not want women entering combat roles. The reasons for this sentiment are numerous and often reflect the opinion of General Barrow; it just is not in a woman's nature to fight and kill. Others include: sexual tension reduces efficiency and creates disciplinary problems on close-quartered ships; war fighting is a physically demanding business and women are not physically qualified; ships are already overcrowded and cannot accommodate extra berthing and bathing facilities for women; and let us not forget the superstition that having a woman aboard a ship is bad luck.

GET OVER IT GUYS! Face the facts. Women can and have fought in battles—from Molly Pitcher in the Revolutionary War to the women warriors of Desert Storm. Sex and sexual tension may create problems initially. Yet the Navy is an organization of regulations and forbids sex on duty. Aboard ship you are on duty twenty-four hours a day and each command is capable of enforcing discipline. The physical demands of war fighting decrease as weapon technology increases. Today only 1 percent of Navy jobs (underwater explosive ordinance demolition) are too strenuous for the well-conditioned military woman. Ships will require modifications to provide separate berthing for women. However, the Pentagon has stated that ships built after 1975 are easily modified. Pre-1975 ships can be retrofitted when they go to shipyards for scheduled overhaul.

Former Secretary of Defense Les Aspin and President Clinton have opened combat positions for women. The Pentagon's goal is to increase the percentage of women in the Navy from 10.5 percent today to 15 percent by 1999. The change in roles will require adjustments. The most difficult adjustments will not be ship retrofits or weight training for women. They will be adjustments in attitudes. With these changing attitudes will come realizations. Realizations that women can add to the efficiency and morale of combat squadrons and ships. Commands that welcome the integration of women, demand equal and fair treatment throughout the chain of command, and deal with problems openly and swiftly, will quickly adjust to and benefit from the changing face of the Navy.

In 2016, the United States military opened all jobs in all services to women. Yet, females still make up less than 20 percent of the Navy and less than 1 percent of thirteen ratings. I am not sure why this is. I am sure that quotas are not the solution, if there even is or needs to be one.

As my separation date from the Navy approached, the question of what to do next became more pressing. I needed a plan. I paid $1,500 to take a course and get my airline transport pilot license. Busman and I flew the check flight together in a twin-engine Beechcraft Duchess with an instructor. Patricia thought it would be fun to ride along in the fourth seat. As I executed steep climbs, stall recoveries, and other maneuvers required to pass the check ride, and the instructor pulled engines and simulated other emergencies, Patricia started turning green around the gills. We dropped her off at the terminal before switching seats so that Busman could complete his check ride. We both passed and I submitted applications to all the major airlines. But in the early 1990s they were going through tough economic times and furloughing pilots, not hiring them.

My aerospace engineering degree was dated, and computers had advanced a bit beyond the hole-punched cards we fed into giant machines at Georgia Tech to solve simple equations. More importantly, I still did not want to be an engineer. I went to a seminar with Prudential Insurance, but they pitched selling policies to all your family and friends, which did not interest me. Patricia had a well-paying job at Nissan, so going back to school was an option, although I would need more student loans. I still owed on my undergraduate loans, having deferred payment during my military service.

On a bit of a lark, Scott Harders and I decided to take the LSAT (Law School Admission Test). I surprised myself by placing in the ninety-fourth percentile. That, along with strong letters of recommendation from squadron COs and Capt. Braden, balanced out my 2.5 undergraduate GPA. As a result, I got into Western State and the University of San Diego, but not my school of choice, UCLA. Scott also got into USD and we both decided to enroll.

I flew my last flights as a VAW-110 Firebird at the end of January 1994. I bounced on and off a flight deck with Lt.(jg) Ketchum as he got carrier qualified in the E-2 on Friday, January 28, during the day. That night, I gave an instrument check to Lt.(jg) Peters on a cross-country flight to Hill Air Force Base in Utah. We loaded our skis, boots, and poles into the tube of the E-2 after dark, while the line crew made wisecracks. After skiing Alta Mountain, one of my favorites, on Saturday, we flew home Sunday.

As I hit the break at NAS Miramar that cold, clear afternoon at 350 knots, banked hard left sixty degrees, pulled back firmly on the yoke, and flew my last downwind and approach as a naval aviator, I knew I would miss the job immensely. I did and still do. Thirty years later, I still dream about flying Navy aircraft. Sometimes I am handling an emergency. In other dreams I am simply flying over an endless ocean or the Grand Canyon, where I logged hundreds of hours while the NFOs worked with fighters over the Yuma desert. Occasionally, I am bagging traps aboard a carrier on a sunny day (never at night, which terrified me enough then without having nightmares about it now). There is little that compares to the thrill of piloting a military aircraft, especially on and off a carrier. Although presenting a case to a jury at trial comes close.

Having bid the traditional *fair winds and following seas* to my friends in the Navy, seven months stood ahead before law school classes began. Our son Jack was four months old and Patricia commuted to LA every day to support the family, leaving by six thirty every morning and often getting home after seven at night. That gave me the most down time I had ever had in my life, if you count watching after an infant as down time, which I did. Patricia and I bought a brand-new bright red jogging stroller at the El Toro Marine Station PX and I took Jack on daily runs along the beach.

To save money, we moved into a small two-bedroom apartment on Golden Lantern Street in Dana Point, California. Our apartment overlooked Shipwreck Park, a small sanctuary with a swing set and a handful of other playground attractions. The park was known for drug sales and use after dark. But over the park and down the hill stood Dana Point Harbor, one of the most scenic harbors and marinas in the world.

This will sound sexist, but mothers should care for children, at least infants or at least in my family. Once, while Jack napped on our bed, I ran down the two flights of stairs to the basement to grab the laundry from the dryer. When I got back to the room he was gone! I tossed the laundry basket on the bed and frantically searched. I found him, still asleep, snuggled between the bed and the wall, where he had rolled.

Another time, I decided to wash my Ford Probe after a run along the beach. Jack napped curbside in his stroller at the top of our hill overlooking the harbor. The push button brake on the stroller let loose while I was hosing off the car. I saw the red stroller start to move out of the corner of my eye, dropped the hose, and lunged toward Jack as the stroller hopped the curb into the street. Fortunately, it tipped over instead of racing down the hill into traffic and I was able to grab Jack, who did not sleep through that one. All in all though, we got along well. Plenty of books, games, sing-alongs, baby food, and diapers.

I did not really keep up with my Navy comrades after leaving the service. I got busy with a family and other things, as did they. I went to law school with Scott and talked to Spike and Busman occasionally, once every few years when a Christmas card revealed something noteworthy, but that was about it. Yet I flew out to DC from Colorado and drove down to Patuxent River, Maryland, to attend Spike's retirement in 2010. And Spike drove all night from Pax River to Hilton Head, South Carolina to attend my father's memorial in 2013, turning around and driving home afterward. Having experienced what we have, we realize that talk can be nice, but actions mean much more than words.

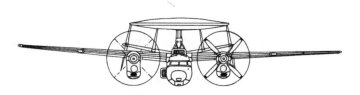

SECTION IV

IN SUMMATION

CHAPTER 16

A BRIEF RECAP OF TWENTY-EIGHT
YEARS IN LAW

I LOVED LAW SCHOOL. AND it turned out I could get good grades when I studied. I ended up as class valedictorian. In giving the valedictory speech, I stressed three virtues my classmates and I should pursue in our work as lawyers: honesty, integrity, and compassion. I noted that "to be a forceful negotiator or zealous advocate, a lawyer need not lack compassion; in fact, I think often the converse is true." I also won several other awards, including the Dean's Award for Legal Scholorship. The typo is not mine; it appears on the plaque I received that proudly, and hilariously, hangs on the wall of my home office, along with a few other prized plaques and awards from my Navy and law careers.

After law school, I spent thirteen years with brilliant attorneys at international law firm Gibson Dunn practicing antitrust, intellectual property, and securities law. In 2010, I got a wonderful job with the United States Securities and Exchange Commission, where I worked as a trial attorney until retiring last March. At the SEC, I litigated and tried cases against individuals and entities accused of fraud and other violations of the securities laws. My colleagues were smart, dedicated, professionals and great fun to work with. As in the Navy, my time as a lawyer provided the opportunity, through hard work, to travel throughout our great country and the world. I met boatloads of wonderful people along the way.

The thing I enjoy most about being a trial attorney is bringing litigation to a close, whether by settlement or resolution by the court or a jury. Settlement is often the better result for all involved. No more money spent to litigate or appeal and, often more importantly, it offers finality. Other times, a trial is required to resolve irreconcilable differences. That is the fun part.

I must tread lightly in discussing my time litigating and trying cases, and I speak on behalf of neither former employer. But I will share a few anecdotes from my first trial at the SEC, all of which is public record.

In early 2011, shortly after I joined the SEC, Chris Friedman, paralegal Joe Murphy, and I put on a jury trial against Dr. Manny Shulman, in Fort Lauderdale, Florida. We alleged that Manny and some cohorts orchestrated a securities scam, issuing false press releases to raise investor funding through an unregistered securities offering. Manny's codefendants settled two weeks before trial. Manny chose to go to trial *pro se* (representing himself), which is almost never a good idea. We had named Manny's wife, Krystal, as a relief defendant, alleging that, while she did not do anything wrong, she had been unjustly enriched through Manny's fraud and should have to repay her ill-gotten gains.

Krystal showed up to the courtroom for trial every day in the shortest of skirts, the highest of heels, and the lowest of necklines, her hair coiffed high and to perfection. I examined her about the family's extravagant expenses for pool maintenance, spa and nail salon visits, and exotic vacations, all funded with investor money. Her obvious annoyance at answering my questions about her lifestyle did not do her any favors with the jury.

We called Manny's former business partner as a witness. He was a doctor, like Manny, who claimed Manny had previously defrauded him in a wellness center scam. He despised Manny, and despite my best efforts during witness preparation, he went off the rails on the witness stand during direct examination. He called Manny a psychopath, among other things, in front of the jury. US District Court Judge for the Southern District of Florida William Zloch sternly ordered me to control my witness. I really did try.

Chris put Steven Thel on the stand on a sultry Southern Florida afternoon as an expert witness. Professor Thel was a knowledgeable and articulate, cigar-chomping professor from Fordham University. He explained to the jury how the registration requirements of the securities laws operate and how those requirements, as well as the laws requiring full disclosure, promote fair and efficient capital markets and protect investors. Following Professor Thel's direct examination, which Chris and Steven deftly handled, Manny cross-examined the professor. Manny's rambling, self-flagellation of a cross-examination only succeeding in digging his hole deeper in front of the jury.

At one point, Judge Zloch got frustrated and asked the witness a question from the bench to try to help Manny along. Following the question, Manny shouted "Objection!" from the podium. He objected to the judge's own question. When Judge Zloch asked Manny the basis for his objection, Manny said something about the witness not telling the whole story. Judge Zloch promptly overruled the objection and had Professor Thel answer his question.

We finished the witnesses on Friday and worked on our closing argument over the weekend. After we presented those on Monday, Judge Zloch read the jury their instructions and sent them to deliberate. The jury came back shortly after lunch with a verdict in our favor on all counts against both the Shulmans.

Chris and I could not celebrate that night, because we had to argue remedies the next day. We further researched the law based upon the jury's findings and prepared until three o'clock that morning, before grabbing a few hours of sleep. Tuesday morning, Chris persuasively argued for Dr. Shulman to have to pay back all the investor funds he illegally raised, pay a significant penalty, and be barred from the securities industry for life. Judge Zloch agreed and so ordered.

The next day, Chris and I rented a sailboat from a beachfront Marriott a quarter mile down the street from the Comfort Inn we had been living and working in for two weeks. We enjoyed a few hours of fun in warm Atlantic waters before flying back to the frigid temperatures of Denver.

Preparing for trial requires an immense amount of work. But when prepared, the thrill of sparring with witnesses and the judge in front of a jury is remarkably fun and rewarding. I hope to do it again someday if the right case comes along.

I have profound respect for our judicial system. Our trial courts, via lawyers, judges, juries, and Constitutional rights to due process, etc., reach a just result in the overwhelming majority of cases. And when unhappy with the result, there is the right to appeal. Unruly mobs protesting rulings they disagree with, often without taking the time to understand the legal arguments involved, are disrespectful and counterproductive. And attempting to intimidate judges is a crime. Such conduct only underscores the importance of the rule of law and an inviolate Constitution.

CHAPTER 17

PARTING THOUGHTS

OUR COUNTRY IS PRESENTLY DANGEROUSLY divided. I blame a biased, unserious media and, as a result, uninformed voters that elect aloof and unaccountable politicians. Term limits would help stem the division and bitter rhetoric that deepens it. COVID-19 should have united us. Instead, the media, big business, and government politicized everything from masks, to shutdowns, schools, and vaccines, creating confusion and even more division.

Regardless, I am an optimist. It is a dreary existence otherwise. In March and April of 2020, I endured two spinal fusion surgeries, followed by a grueling recovery, during the worst global pandemic in one hundred years. The experience offered an opportunity to reflect. The day after Patricia brought me home from the hospital, four days after my second surgery (no visitors, thanks COVID), I called Busman. We talked about what was going on in the country, after catching up about our families and lives. I posted the following after our call:

> I talked with an old Navy friend this morning amidst all the COVID-19 (sing along to the tune of "Come on Eileen!") hubbub. Afterwards I contemplated how we were trained to react to an emergency as a pilot—which requires significantly quicker response time but applies broadly.

1. **Aviate:** do not stall or crash your aircraft because there is a problem, keep flying and evaluate what is wrong.

2. **Navigate:** you are in a dynamic environment—whether in a cockpit or practicing self-isolation, you are someplace and going somewhere—do not abandon that without reason.

3. **Communicate:** let others know what is going on, seek advice or assistance, and make plans to get through the emergency with the help of others.

> It is imperative that these steps be followed in this order. Many an aircraft has stalled, run into a mountain, or even the ground, trying to change course or talk to somebody about a problem rather than addressing the immediate threat. So, take a walk with your spouse, talk to your family and friends, call an elderly neighbor and ask if they need anything from the store. And pray for (and if inclined reach out to) your politicians; ask them to react to this emergency calmly and rationally—please do not fly us into a mountain trying to get on CNN, MSNBC, or Fox News.

I am fearful for our country, where citizens and even elected representatives do not understand or appreciate the beauty of our democratic republic. Or, crucially, a constitution that unites the people of fifty disparate, but cohesive, states. I see signs, however, that the citizenry is waking up, in a good way. Parents become fierce protectors when they realize their children are being harmed and used as political pawns. Businesses, especially small ones, do not support or thrive under vandalism and looting. Americans do not appreciate the higher prices or local business closures that result from such lawless behavior.

Americans also recognize hypocrisy and misdirection, and are coming to realize, hopefully in horror, that they do not want to live in a country where a mob (either online or in person) is unchallenged when it screeches for abandoning due process, freeing criminals, and ideological conformity. It becomes worse when big business and tech giants jump onto the virtue signaling band wagon in the hope that they can sidestep the meandering and metastasizing rage that has abandoned both common sense and civil discourse.

As I lay on the gurney waiting for the anesthesiologist to put me under for the second surgery, I said a prayer. I did not pray to survive the surgery and hospital stay, though I certainly expected and wanted to. I prayed that if something went wrong, my family and my country would be okay.

We are all going to die. We seem to forget that. Enjoy the time God gives you. Celebrate with family, friends, and strangers. Mourn when appropriate. Protest when necessary. Fight when required. Live and love while you can. Do your best. Try to help. Do not be afraid to make mistakes; but when you do, own them. Do not judge yourself or others too harshly, or worry too much about what others think or say about you. Be kind. Perhaps most importantly, have fun.

No one can solve all the world's problems or change human nature. But we can all work toward improvement and avoid senseless destruction. This realization comforted me as the anesthesiologist squeezed the drugs into my intravenous line. I am lucky. Patricia and I have been able to provide for our family and others. Each of our three children got a good (although too politically biased) education and are responsible young adults. I am immensely proud of each of them. I have a fantastic marriage to a wonderful wife I adore. I live on an amazing planet, in a beautiful country, state, county, city, and home. I am relatively healthy, given the mileage. I am happy.

One reason for that happiness is I do not harbor regrets or animosities, at least not for long. I do not regret having to work hard for what I could afford; it made me appreciate it. I am glad Stanford, Duke, Rice, and Virginia rejected me; I got a better education and made lifelong friends at Georgia Tech. I do not regret incurring debt to attend Georgia Tech and the USD School of Law; it incentivized me to choose marketable degrees and study hard. I also do not regret having to pay back that debt over two decades; it taught me the importance of money, and what it can and cannot provide. I am not angry about spending a few nights in jail; I mostly deserved it. I hold no grudges against the friend or fellow flight instructor that turned me in to the Tailhook commission (though I regret my conduct); I am stronger for it and learned a valuable lesson. Slamming on and off carrier decks for eight years likely had something to do with my back issues, but I would not change that for the world. Life, be it brief or a hundred years, is too short to dwell on anger or grudges. In the beautifully sung words of Elsa from the movie *Frozen*: "Let it go!"

Too many today focus on the sins of slavery and oppression committed by the United States in the past (sins also committed by every other nation on earth), while glossing over our country's many great triumphs and achievements. Some seek to persecute the Little Sisters of the Poor because they resist being forced to provide contraceptives, and Christian bakers that refuse to create cakes celebrating same sex marriages. Why? Will forcing someone else to go against their beliefs make either you or them happy? I doubt it.

Rather than attack or dictate to others, we should self-reflect and seek forgiveness for our own sins. As importantly, we must find a way to forgive those who trespass against us. Many loud voices have an unhealthy focus on exacting retribution for any offense, especially against those who fail to share their "truths," which often replace a rejected religion. But we must all realize we are not God. The world is much bigger than any individual or group. We are created in God's image, but we are each flawed, mortal, humans. Thus, we should largely leave the burden of judging others to an omniscient, eternal being. By realizing and indeed embracing our mortality and flaws, asking forgiveness for our sins, and giving thanks to the god (or other higher power or fortuitous happpenstance) that granted us the gift of life, we can find happiness.

When I die, which I will, I plan to do so having sincerely sought forgiveness for my many sins and having forgiven all those who have trespassed against me. In so doing, I hope to traverse into the loving embrace of the Father, Son, and Holy Spirit. I may be wrong about the afterlife. I am a relatively smart guy, and one thing I know for certain is that I am often wrong. But if I am, I will be dead. It will not much matter. Regardless, hopefully, by trying to lead a life such that Saint Peter would, perhaps begrudgingly, let me slip through the gates of heaven, I will have left the world I inhabited for a brief time a better place. When I look at my children, I know that at least in that regard I have.

I have led a fun and fulfilling life. I plan to continue to do so for many years to come. Marriages, births, birthdays, anniversaries, holidays, and other events and adventures await. I look forward to spending loads of time with my beloved Patricia and hanging around our kids, and someday grandkids—to the point of annoyance.

For those who have hung in until the end (or peeked ahead), I will share some advice I gave to each of my children in letters I wrote them, hoping they would take some of it and it would help them lead a happy life:

1. Always treat others how you would have them treat you. (Borrowed that from Jesus.)

2. Expect everybody to follow #1, but do not be naïve about it.

3. Seize the day, but plan for the future.

4. Always be thankful for the many blessings bestowed upon you.

5. Make it a point to give to charity in at least a couple of ways every year—and do your homework, the ACLU only supports approved liberties and just handing over money or even food to people is not always an effective way to help.

6. Self-reflection is time well spent, as is praying.

7. It is more important that a spouse be easy on the ears than the eyes, but you can have both.

8. Question facts and assumptions drawn from those facts, and do not confuse the two.

9. Do not let others tell you or anybody else what to think or say. Everyone should be heard and can try to persuade, but no one can dictate.

10. Pick your battles wisely, win them fairly or lose with grace, and move on.

Wishing each of you fair winds and following seas.

EPILOGUE

TOWARD THE END OF MY time at Gibson Dunn, I occupied a west-facing office on the forty-first floor of the opulent Qwest building in downtown Denver, Colorado—1801 California Street, for those who know the area. One of many great mentors, managing partner George Curtis, officed to the southwest in a bigger office with a better view of the Rocky Mountains. George walked in one afternoon to discuss an upcoming trial.

He asked about at a framed picture I had recently hung on my wall. The close-up photograph captures an E-2C Hawkeye pulling up at maximum airspeed and g-force into a gray sky above a placid ocean. White contrails spin off the tips of the wings as they bend and strain against the dew-soaked air to gain altitude. I explained that the photograph captured Spike and me pulling up in front of the *Connie* in the CVW-14 air demo we flew for our fathers on Tiger Cruise.

Affixed to the bottom left corner of the glass, with a piece of yellowed Scotch tape, is a birthday card Patricia gave me. A sepia toned photograph shows a boy in a leather helmet and goggles sitting in a go-cart. He has just launched into the sky off a twin-railed metal ramp. The card carries the inscription:

Life is either a daring adventure, or nothing at all.

The quote is from Helen Keller.

Can you imagine such a statement from a deaf, mute, and blind girl born in a country without the freedoms, values, and innovations of the United States of America?

Spike and I fly the E-2C in the Tiger Cruise Airshow

ACKNOWLEDGMENTS

THANKS TO EACH OF MY children for reading initial drafts and providing helpful feedback, fellow shipmates that checked my recollections for accuracy, and my lovely wife Patricia, who provided sound advice, along with much love and support throughout the journey of writing this book and living my life.

And thanks to the editing and design teams at Köehler Books for their great work in bringing this project to fruition.

LETTERS HOME

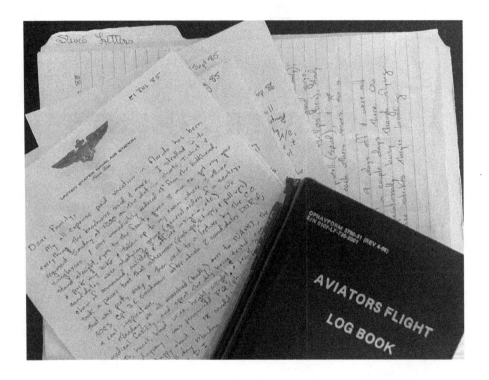

In settling my parents' affairs, I discovered a faded manila folder labeled "Steve's Letters" in my mother's cursive. The folder contained over ninety pages of real-time observations from some of the farthest reaches of the planet and inspired "Fair Winds, Following Seas, and a Few Bolters." Using these, my log books, and other sources, I began writing. My third letter home from AOCS, as well as my first from the *Connie* cruise and second from the *Indy* are reproduced in the following pages.

19 Aug 85

Dear Family,

First of all I'd like to thank you all for the many thoughtful & interesting letters. I only wish I could find the time to write back more often. They weren't kidding when they said the pace picked up after the first couple weeks.

Our class has really been catching a lot of flak from the D.I. & everyone else for being a "dirtball" class & to tell you the truth there are several candidates who I would classify as such. The fact that 4 candidates failed the 4th week RLP (if they fail again they're attrited) & it only takes one to make a formation look bad & we have 4 or 5 we've started out on the wrong foot. GYSGT Crenshaw has isolated 5 who he's really been riding to DOR. We've P.T.'d everyday this week in khakis in his passageway until drenched. He does things like take the one who screws up (one of the 5) & has them stand up & call the up-downs while the rest of the class does push-ups for them. He's quite good at creating dissention. I only participated Monday though as Tuesday I had some fluid drained from my elbow. No big deal but I'm on light duty till Friday & can't do push-ups.

We ran the obstacle course Monday & it was exhausting. I qualified (passed) & missed the time for PT award by 21 sec. I & slipped off the monkey bars once so I think I'll be able to PT it, especially after training. We ran the cross-country course yesterday (I got permission to run & drill) & I ran the 1.6 miles w/ sand in 9:26, 4 seconds off PT time. 5th in the class & pretty good for someone who hates to run. Academics is also going well. I have a 97 average so far on 8 tests & we haven't even started the big 3 (Aero, Engines, & Navigation) yet, in which my engineering background should be a big advantage. In drill we have 3 squads & I'm the 3rd squad leader. See Dad when I get motivated I do pretty well.

Next week (the 6th) is a biggee. The other classes say it is the hardest of the 14. I have Mate of the Deck (watch) duty Sat. for 24 hrs. Monday is the Law final, Tues. the Seapower final & phase one of the swimming tests (tower jump & treading & drownproofing in full flight gear). Wednesday is the RLP inspection at 0700 & then the mile swim in flight gear. We will also be starting Aero & Engines, drilling, & running the O & X-C courses. I sure hope we pass the RLP so I can have a beer after that week.

I spent a whole lot of money the other day ordering uniforms ~ $650 but since that should cover my entire wardrobe & I don't have anything else to spend money on I figured it wouldn't hurt.

Martha came down last Sunday & visited for a couple hours. It was nice to see her but would've been nicer to be able to go to the beach or something.

It's time for me to polish my brass & boots now & do some studying so I will bid you all adieu.

> Love & miss you all,
> Steve

Bobby & Pete: Thanks for the letter & I hope you enjoy your convention & sightseeing in D.C.

Sarah: Thanks again for the cookies & for the letter

Mom: Thank you for the plethera of munchies

Kathy: Thanks for the letter & I can't wait to see you Phil & the nephew again soon. Tell me how Phil likes the new job when he gets settled.

Dad: Thanks for the letter. Yes they do still call it pogey-bait. And if you want details on graduation now you're going to have to tell it to the Marines.

Dear Family,

Well, we're underway & headed west now. CQ (carrier qualification) was hectic but we finally managed to get all pilots qual'ed day & night except me. I still need to get a night trap. This is alright because to get a night qualification trap you must first get a day trap so I've been bagging a day trap every day to be ready for when I get into the night pattern. With traps being fairly scarce this serves to get me more than my share. The deck has been pitching pretty well in 8-10 ft swells the last couple of days making getting aboard tricky.

Things have settled down after the first couple days at sea & everyone is getting used to the idea of being here awhile. Our 6-man stateroom is set up nicely w/ a stereo & CD player, 2 small TV's, a refrigerator (for sodas only), & a MacIntosh. My roommates are all good guys, Darryl Long (Spike), Adam Ferreira (DucknEdge), Curtis Phillips (Otis), Andy Dressel (Sausage), & Wes Spidell (Spud), & we shouldn't start getting on each others nerves for a while yet.

Hawaii is only 9 days off & we're all looking forward to a couple days there. On the way we're operationally busy though flying st against practice strikes they're launching against us from Hawaii. It's a little different flying when you're over 500 nm from any land & the carrier is the only place you can land. This is called "blue water ops." We almost had to barricade an A-6 last night who kept boltering (missing all the arresting wires), but on his last pass before barricade after sucking the tanker dry he snagged a 1 wire. A barricade is when you rig a net (a strong one) across the flight deck & catch the plane that way. It's pretty dangerous though & can damage the aircraft even if all goes well so it's only used as a last resort.

We're flying all night tonight trying to find the strike force that's attacking us & I've got LSO duty so it'll be a long one. Gotta go catch the birds now. Take care.

Love,
Steve

P.S. Well I was going to make this about how clear the night was & how many stars were out but that didn't matter when an EA-6B didn't come back to the ship this morning. We're not sure where it is & it's out of gas by now. We'll fly all night/morning on a SAR (search & rescue) & hopefully pick up a radio beacon & pick up the crew of 4 in the morning. Gonna grab an hour of sleep now before the next recovery. Good night.

USS INDEPENDENCE
CV-62

31 July 90

Dear Mom & Dad,

Hello from the Indian Ocean. Everything is fine here on the Independence. Today was the crossing the line ceremonies as we crossed the equator & all slimy wogs were initiated into the royal order of trusty shellbacks. Having been across last cruise hence being a shellback I participated in the administering of the initiation rites as opposed to recieving. Definitely the preferred way to go through a crossing the line ceremony. It's all in fun but it does kind of resemble fraternity Hell Week. Basically the wogs spend a few hours getting good & slimy via eggs, coffee, butter, & anything else you can get out of the mess deck garbage. They're brought before a kangaroo court

USS INDEPENDENCE
CV-62

& charged with various crimes. When they plead not guilty they drink truth serum (you don't want to know what's in it). After this & some other fun & games they are brought to an elevator & taken up to the flight deck where they kiss the royal baby. That's the belly of the fatest chief all slopped up with garbage. They then jump in the tank of knowledge & our shellbacks. Am I really 28 & a professional pilot?

We had a tragedy a week ago when an A-6 was lost on a night bombing exercise. Apparently they impacted the water as their wingman & a few other aircraft in the area saw the fireball. We flew the next day as planned. It's strange how it didn't

USS INDEPENDENCE
CV-62

seem to affect the crew much. People were a little somber for a while but by lunch the next day even the A-6 guys seemed to be joking around as usual. It's hard to justify loss of life out here but I guess it could've happened just as easily on the beach. A memorial service was held 2 days after the accident which was well done & widely attended. I didn't know either the pilot or BN very well.

We won't be pulling into any ports for a while except for 2 days in Diego Garcia.

Give my love to everyone & it's always great to hear from you.

Love,
Steve

192

GLOSSARY

OF MILITARY ACRONYMS

AEW	Airborne early warning
AMDO	Aviation maintenance duty officer
AOCS	Aviation Officer Candidate School
BOQ	Bachelor Officers' Quarters
CAG	Carrier Air Group; also colloquial for the CAG commander
CAPC	Carrier aircraft plane commander
CAPT.	Captain (Navy O-6) Captain (Marine O-3)
CDR.	Commander (Navy O-5)
CIC	Combat Information Center
CINCPAC	Commander in chief, Pacific fleet
CO OR SKIPPER	Commanding officer
COD	Carrier onboard delivery aircraft—C-2 Greyhound
COMNAVAIRPAC	Commander Naval Air Pacific
CPO	Chief petty officer (Navy E-7)
CQ	Carrier qualification
CV(N)	Aircraft carrier (Nuclear)
CVW	Carrier air wing
DI	Drill instructor

DOR	Drop on request
ENS.	Ensign (Navy O-1)
FAA	Federal Aviation Administration
FCLP	Field carrier landing practice
GONZO	Gulf of Oman Naval Zone of Operations
GY.SGT.	Gunnery sergeant (Marine E-7)
IFR	Instrument flight rules
JO	Junior officer (O-1 to O-3)
LSO	Landing signals officer
LT.	Lieutenant (Navy O-3)
LT. CDR.	Lieutenant commander (Navy O-4)
LT.(JG)	Lieutenant junior grade (Navy O-2)
NAMI	Naval Aerospace Medical Institute
NAS	Naval Air Station
NATOPS	Naval Aviation Training and Operating Procedures Standardization
NCOIC	Non-commissioned officer in charge
NFO	Naval flight officer
PI	Philippine Islands or the Philippines
PO	Petty officer (Navy E-4 to E-6)
PT	Physical training
RAG	Replacement Air Group
VFR	Visual flight rules
XO	Executive officer

REFERENCES

Chapter 5

Fighter Jets World, "Here is a List of All Blue Angels Accidents: Blue Angels Crash Videos" (June 23, 2018): https://fighterjetsworld.com

America's Navy, "E-2 Hawkeye Airborne Command and Control Aircraft" (last updated: 17 Sep 2021): https://www.navy.mil

Chapter 8

"Navy Investigates Accident In Which Missile Hits Indian Freighter," AP News (December 13, 1988): https://apnews.com

Naval History and Heritage Command, U.S. Navy Seabee Museum, "Cubi Point: They Moved a Mountain," February 26, 2020): https://www.history.navy.mil

Chapter 10

Weebly.com, "Roman Rituals," https://religiousbeliefsofrome.weebly.com

Cameron, A. (1981). *Daughters of Copper Woman*. (Vancouver, BC: Press Gang Publishers).

Chapter 11

John Harper, "Eagle vs Dragon: How the U.S. and Chinese Navies Stack Up," National Defense Magazine (March 9, 2020) https://www.nationaldefensemagazine.org

Chapter 14

Shannon Collins, "Desert Storm: A Look Back," US Department of Defense (January 11, 2019) https://www.defense.gov

Chapter 15

Geoff Ziezulewicz and Mark D. Faram, "Despite changes, 13 Navy ratings are still 99 percent men," Navy Times (August 16, 2017): https://www.navytimes.com

Additional source materials:

USS *Constellation* CV-64 WESTPAC '88-89, cruise book

Department of the Navy, "LSO Reference Manual" (Change 3, July 1990)

United States Navy Aviators Flight Log Books, assigned to Lt. Stephen C. McKenna, OPNAVFORM 3780-31 (Rev 4-05) S/N 0107-LF-736-2001

Lt. McKenna's official Department of Defense Service Record

Printed in the USA
CPSIA information can be obtained
at www.ICGtesting.com
LVHW101622040823
754219LV00004B/443